Psychics, Mediums & Ghost Stories

True Tales of the Supernatural

By

Edward Kwiatkowski

ISBN: 0-7596-8654-8 Ebook
ISBN: 0-7596-8655-6 Softcover

This book is printed on acid free paper.

1stBooks - rev. 05/06/02

ACKNOWLEDGMENTS

I am deeply grateful to the following individuals who were willing to share their mediumistic experiences with me. Without them this book would not have been possible, for I ran out of personal stories with enough word content necessary to make a book complete: Lorraine Brukley, Ruth Chavey, Elizabeth Clemens, Addie Davis, Mike Deradorian, Rita Domenick, June Flowers, Kurt Flowers, Mary Ann Glover, Stephen Gordon, Blaine Johnson II, Jon Kwiat, Marianne Peltz, Ralph Rehmer, Rigo Vega, and Floyd Keeton.

I give special thanks to my son, Edward Kwiatkowski II, who induced interest into the stories with his art work, and my other family members Mary and Maria, who contributed to my thought and word assembling.

My appreciation to the many anonymous tour members who listened to my ghost experiences on my bus tours when I was a tour director with "Tour of the Month", out of Milwaukee, Wisconsin. These were the first people to suggest and encouraged me to put my stories into a book. Thank you all!

CONTENTS

INTRODUCTION

You can't see the wind, but you can feel the wind's presence.
You can't see a spirit, but you may feel a spirit's presence.

You can't see either one, yet they are there.
The wind can be powerful, and so can a spirit.

From where does the wind come?
From where does a spirit come?

The wind can come from any direction, from the east, west
south, north or any part of the world
A spirit can come from any direction, the attack, closet,
bedroom, basement or any part of the house.

When will the wind show up? You're never sure.
When will a spirit show up? You never know.
Yet we accept the wind. Why shouldn't we accept the spirit?
The wind is living out there. Why can't a spirit?

If you want to find out about death, you go to the person who
has had a near death experience.

If you want to find out about ghosts, you go to a person who
has had a ghost occurrence.

You pray - to whom? You get a miracle from whom?

You don't believe in life after death, and you come in contact with someone
from after death - a ghost! Then you believe what science has yet to prove. You
help science believe when you have made a ghost contact.

Here are some stories of ghost connections to think about, if you haven't had
your own.

Ed Kwiatkowski

Dad/Figure 1

DAD

My first personal contact with the supernatural, or what we commonly call "ghosts" was with my father. I went to bed at 10:00 PM, which was early for me. In this bedroom was an extremely heavy, old, wardrobe made of oak. It was heavier than an upright piano or a cast iron stove, and if you're old enough to have had the opportunity to move one of these items, you would know what I mean. Otherwise, believe me it was very heavy! One of the foundations of this story is understanding this fact or nothing will be comprehensible.

During the '20s and '30s, many homes were built without closets, consequently, people used these wardrobes instead. Our home at this time did, but we kept it as a memory of my father who passed away in an army hospital in Wisconsin when I was four years old, and my brother Art one and a half years old. My father was bayoneted in the chest and gassed in World War I, which developed into lung problems and led to his demise.

I knew my father vaguely, but I do remember running down the street with my pudgy legs pumping, my arm extended to hand my father a pack of cigarettes as he was coming home from work. He would then lift me and hug me.

I also remember that when he died, he was laid out in our living room rather than in a funeral parlor. You must remember they did things differently back then. It was even a custom to photograph the loved ones in this last state by a professional photographer if you could afford it. Most families could not because of the Depression, and available "box" cameras were not suited for indoor photography.

On one of the nights he was laid out, I recall being put to bed early. I could hear two young ladies talking near the casket. One of them said in a frightened voice, "Oh I saw him move! Let's get out of here!", and they quickly left. I fell asleep, woke up later, and didn't hear anyone about. I got up to see my Dad, although my mother said that my father was sleeping and he might never get up, but, because the ladies said he moved, I decided to get up to play with him.

As I walked to the casket, no one was around, and I thought he was sleeping again. I got on the kneeler, shook my father, took hold of his crossed hands, and tried to awaken him. Nothing happened, so I went back to sleep. From that day on I was never afraid or squeamish about touching a dead person.

After my father was buried I never thought about him; my whole concern was for my mother, because she would awake me with her crying during the stillness of the night. We lost our home due to a mortgage foreclosure as we were in the midst of a Depression and jobs were not available. When she would find some housework, she could not take it for she had nobody to tend to Art and me. Another factor was that she could not speak English to seek help. Life was unstable for us. We were constantly moving. Our life was full of uncertainties until Art became of school age. It allowed our mother to find work in a cigar factory. Our "baby sitters" became our grade school and the Boys' Club of Detroit. At the age of thirteen my mother remarried, bought a home, and a year later our step-father Victor died of cancer of the throat.

The home they bought was on Pittsburg Street in Detroit. It was a block away from a very busy street with a lot of truck traffic. Many a time our home would vibrate because of it. Other than this, there weren't any other factors to disclaim the circumstances of the story I am about to unfold.

It was 1941, when I was 15 years old that my father came back into my life for just one day. As previously mentioned, it was a hot summer night, and I went to bed about 10:00 PM. My mother was now working afternoons, 4:00 PM to 12:00 AM. My brother Art was not around - or at least I assumed that he wasn't.

I was restless and couldn't fall asleep. I was just tossing and turning. I had the bedroom window open trying to capture some summer breeze, but it was too calm. The only things I captured were the train whistles from the train tracks which were about one and a half miles away. Listening to those sounds, I began to hear another sound which was coming from the old wardrobe stored in my bedroom. It was a rocking sound, which I never heard at any other time. This bothered me for there was no reason for it. There weren't any traffic noises emitting from McGraw Avenue, which was used by trucks going to Kelsey Hayes Wheel Company, three blocks away. With the window open, I would be able to hear them, but I had neither breeze nor vibrations to cause this rocking. I could no longer take it! It affected me like a dripping faucet would! I jumped out of bed to level it. Maybe someone moved it, which I doubted very much, because my mother wasn't capable of moving it. It was so heavy, I used to have to help her. I shoved it from various angles, but it stood steady as the "Rock of Gibralter".

I returned back to bed, and it started its rocking noise again. I figured it had to be Art hiding inside it, trying to be funny. I jumped out of bed again, put on the lights, and quickly opened the wardrobe doors, only to find it empty. I was perplexed. I went back to bed wishing it wouldn't happen again. I was very still, but the rocking noise returned.

Once more I got up, to move it to another spot. I pulled it out slightly, and when I tried to rock it, it was stable. I sat down in the chair next to my bed, staring at it, daring it to rock. Sure enough, it was rocking again. My head was whirling with reasons and ideas which I disappointingly rejected. If someone else was around I would have asked them but I was alone. I am mentally talking to myself, why is this happening—what is the earthly reason—somebody has to be doing this—there must be an answer but what is the answer? Now there is a lapse in the rocking. Why? I got back into bed. It rocked again! I got up and readjusted

2

it. I said to myself; 'This is my father's wardrobe; could it be he wants to communicate with me? What would he want to tell me, and about what? About whom? Eleven years later?' It was quiet then; but I continued my thoughts.

I directed my thoughts to the wardrobe. 'Dad do you want to talk to me?' It rocked! It must be a yes! 'Is it about me?' Silence! 'Is it about Art?' Silence! 'Is it about Ma?' It rocked! 'Now it's about Ma.' What could it be? I thought of my conversation with my mother the previous day.

She was being courted by two fellows, one was John, the other Andy. John was a playboy, very good looking. Andy was quiet - very, very quiet. You never knew what he was thinking. He didn't have much to say, and was not attractive at all. He was skinny and balding. He seemed harmless and shy. My mother asked me with which one should she go steady and maybe marry. My answer was Andy, because he seemed the type that was more of a "home body", more than John. She told me Art gave her the same answer.

I was thinking about my mother's questioning this decision and of its importance in my mother's life. So I said, "Does it have to do with Ma's choice of men?" And it rocked again, and then silence! I said, "All right! Do you think my choice of Andy was correct?" There was silence! "Do you think John would better for her?" I heard rocking for Yes! "That means that you think John is better than Andy. Art's and my choice was Andy. Then you must think that Andy's not the right choice." Again it rocked yes and stopped. "Then Ma should not marry Andy." It vibrated yes! "Ok", I said. "Pa, I will tell Ma that I changed my mind. I will not tell her what has happened here."

The following morning, I just bluntly started the conversation by saying, "Well Ma, I don't know, Andy is all right, but there is something about him that is bothering me. He's too quiet. He could be a deceiving kind of person. I think John would be better for you." She looked at me surprisingly and said, "Why do you think that now?" Oh, I just gave it more thought. I think you would be happier with John, because he is such an outgoing guy. Maybe he is ready to settle down, and won't be a playboy anymore. Maybe, you are the one he needs, the right person. Maybe he will change or you will change him. Look how you changed Victor; he was an alcoholic, and he changed. Remember how happy you were." She said, "Well, I already committed myself to Andy! I told John not to see me anymore."

My mother did marry Andy six months later, and the marriage turned out to be a disaster, just as my father tried to warn me. Andy was an alcoholic, didn't want to be clean, didn't want to go anywhere, wouldn't help with house payments, and would only give her $20 dollars a week towards room and board.

After working all week, my mother would look forward to going shopping or to the popular Sunday picnics, but her lot was to have to stay at home while he drank himself to sleep. He never contributed in any way to her happiness. He never, never made any effort to change.

Art's and my pleas for her to divorce him fell on "deaf ears", because she felt it was morally wrong and disgraceful. Divorce was also looked at with disapproval by our community. I guess only a person living in the 1940s would understand this. Yes, I told her she shouldn't adhere to the mores of others, because they didn't pay her bills nor did they share her sorrows.

I guess all this wouldn't have happened if my mother didn't try to give Art and me a father, or if I would have been more emphatic about my father's directions or if I would have been more convincing to my mother, I would not have failed neither him nor her!

Little Man/Figure 2

LITTLE MAN

He was the tiniest baby. He was the shortest in his grade school class. He was the shortest in his division when he was in the army in World War II. He was surprised he got into the service. He was inducted because it was the tail end of the war. The army was desperate for replacements due to the many casualties.

They started to take married men with two or three children, which was unheard of before. Some had major medical problems that would be overlooked. I had low blood pressure, and they took me! In his case it was being very short, too short, which they ignored! His rifle was slightly shorter than he.

At this time in 1945, there was a joke going around about an army inductee who had no arms. He asked the sergeant what good was he to the army with no arms. The sergeant replied, "See that soldier pumping water into a bucket, you tell him when it is full for he is blind."

His mother, of course, mothered him probably more than other mothers mothered their child. She also was very protective of him because he was so small, and ridiculed for this. He was also very shy. All this made her a very doting mother.

The mother herself was a very large and heavy person. She would escort him to and from school to look after his safety. Many of the school children would tease and pester him with obnoxious remarks. She was his shield as much as possible from any harm.

She was always very, very concerned about his welfare. When he went to sleep, she would always wait to make sure that he fell asleep before doing anything else. She would then go up the stairs to his bedroom as quietly as her weight permitted to check on him, and lightly kiss him on the cheek or forehead.

In high school, and after returning from service, he participated in all the social activities available. He attended many many dances in the neighborhood in order to meet someone to date. But, he was always chosen last or not at all. He was what we used to call back then a "wall flower". If he was ever chosen, it was because a girl herself was not picked, she loved to dance, and it didn't matter with whom. He could never make any solid relationships. Everyone looked at him as a little boy, even though he was equal or older in age.

When he became 52 years old, his mother passed away. A week after the funeral he went to the movies. Upon his return he climbed the stairs, got into bed, and did not immediately fall asleep. He heard some one coming up the stairs, because they creaked so loudly even if someone was not heavy. In this case it sounded like his mother, even though she had passed away. But of course, she passed away! How could it be her? Slowly, the steps came toward him, each step creaking.

It was totally dark, so he could not make out who it was or what it was. The first thing that came to his mind, was that it must be his father. The steps continued to the side of his bed. All of a sudden, he felt a light kiss on his cheek, such as previously done by his mother. He laid there listening as the footsteps proceeded away from him, and down the squeaking steps. As the sounds faded away, he jumped out of bed, and ran down the stairs. At the same time his father came out of his room. They both looked at each other, and returned to their rooms without saying a word for they both understood.

Could both have had the same dream? I doubt it! It is my belief that spirits return when there is closeness in the family, to comfort them, and to relate to them that everything is satisfactory.

Mary Ann/Figure 3

MARY ANN

It was years ago, back in the 1960s when I was almost fourteen. It was a very beautiful day, no sight of rain. I went to my girl friend's house that day. The family invited me to take a ride with them to Hell, Michigan. But first I had to let my parents know, and to see if it was okay.

At first they didn't like the idea, that I would be going so far away from home. Since my mother knew the family real well, she gave in. I couldn't be more happy, knowing I was going to have the fun of my life.

My girlfriend Linda, her family and I took off for the day. I was so excited, because I had never been outside of Detroit. It seemed like such a great adventure, if only for a day.

Linda and I were happily enjoying the beautiful scenery, talking and singing at times. She and I grew up together, and have been friends for a long time, we felt as if we were sisters. If we weren't together, we felt like something was wrong. The only thing that would keep us apart was if one was sick.

Going there it seemed as if we would never get there. Linda's younger sister and brother were getting mighty fussy being in the car so long. Finally we made it, and everyone was glad to get out of the car, but for Linda and me, it was a relaxing trip and special.

Special, because her father had the nicest car around. It was a big black Buick. He always kept it waxed so shiny that you could see your face in it. I loved that car, because my family never owned a car. We rode on busses if we had any place to go. I always looked forward to riding in that big black Buick.

It was 1:00 P.M. when we arrived. It was like another world. The grass was so green. You could see flowers blooming everywhere. Everyone ran in different directions to see the countryside. Linda's mother and father were getting things out of the car - blankets, coolers, cold drinks and packed lunches for all.

We kids were a wee bit hungry, so we all joined in to help bring all the food from the car for a lovely picnic. We had so much to eat - fried chicken, potato salad, pop, chips and even dessert. To me it was more like a big feast. We kept eating until we couldn't eat another bite. Then we all lay down to rest a while.

After resting for a while, we all took a walk. It was such a lovely day, with a cool breeze in the air. There were walking trails in every direction. Linda and I ran trying to leave the little ones behind. Her parents called us back, because they didn't want us separated, for we might get lost.

The sun shone so brilliantly through the trees that day. As we walked the trails, we saw rabbits, deer, pheasants, and even a woodchuck. We came to a stream from which we all drank the cold refreshing water. It tasted so good after our long walk.

We sat down for a bit. Linda's father, Mr. Ash, got his fishing rod, and we all took turns trying to catch a fish. But no luck! It was starting to get dark. We headed back to the car. It was near total darkness when we got back to it. We gathered everything, and put it in the trunk of the car.

Now it was total darkness as we headed back home. Linda's father, in his eagerness to get us home before it got too late, made a wrong turn. The road we were on was pitch dark, because we were going through a heavily wooded area. We kept going and going without any cars or street lights in sight. The only lights we had were our headlights. I noticed the name of the road we were on, it was called Knock Knock.

There weren't any houses around, except for one in the far distance. We got to about three city blocks from it when the car went dead. Mr. Ash got out of the car with his flashlight, and lifted the hood to see what was wrong. He discovered he was out of gas.

He walked to the house with all its lights on. He knocked several times. Suddenly all the lights went out. Nobody came to the door! Mr. Ash came back, and told us we would have to spend the night sleeping in the car. In the morning he would go back to the house to see if someone would answer the door. He said, they probably were afraid to answer the door to a stranger this late at night.

We locked all the car doors, talked a little while, and finally we fell asleep. I don't know how long I slept, or what time it was when I felt the car moving from side to side as if in slow motion. I was too scared to even look up. I shook Linda and her sister and brother to no avail. No one would get up! It seemed like it would never stop. I was too petrified to scream. The shaking gradually stopped. I never did look up. I only huddled in the corner of the back seat. I couldn't wait for morning. Finally it was daybreak, when slowly, one by one, they started to get up.

I told them what had happened when they were sleeping, and how I tried to wake them, but couldn't. They said I must have been dreaming, but I knew I wasn't.

Mr. Ash said he would try to start the car one more time before he would go up to the house again. He turned the ignition key on, and to his and our amazement it started. I was so happy. I just wanted to get away from that place.

Mr. Ash was perplexed, he couldn't figure out why it did start. Last night it wouldn't, and the gas tank gauge was on empty. This morning it started, plus the gasoline gauge went up to half full.

With these troubling thoughts we headed back home. We got back on our "empty" gasoline tank. Everyone was no longer skeptical of my ghostly experience, only mystified.

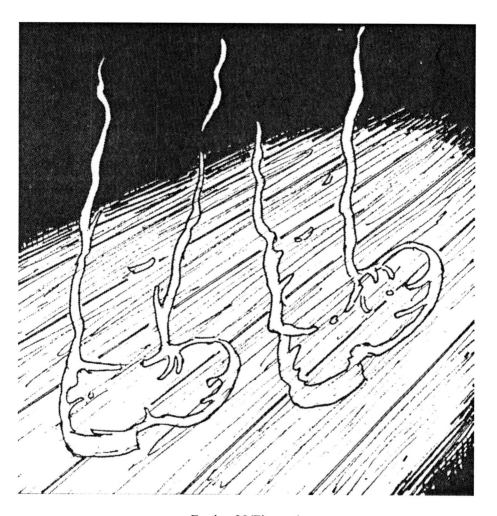

Engine 29/Figure 4

ENGINE 29

On the Detroit Fire Department there are always a lot of pranks being played. For example, the most used and favorite of all practical jokes was the story of "Moe". This jest was saved for the new fire fighters or "trial men", who were told that on their night watch, they would have to be careful of Moe. The description of Moe, went something like this:

"He carries with him a deep hatred of fire fighters. This hatred developed because he blames all fire fighters for having been slow in responding and having been negligent in saving him and his parents at their house fire. The result being, that his parents were killed in the fire, while he was left with a disfigured face and hands. Now, seeking revenge, there's no telling when he would show up."

Having set up a "rookie" with this tale. The fire fighters in on this "joke" would assign him a night watch, and gleefully execute their plan. One of the guys would put on old clothing and a hideous mask. He would walk dragging his foot and carrying a butcher knife toward the new firefighter, saying repeatedly, "I'm gonna get you! I'm Moe! I'm gonna kill ya!" Hair standing on end, most new firefighters would take off running upstairs to the dormitory to wake up everyone to warn them of Moe's arrival, only to be greeted by empty beds, because everyone was downstairs. They came out of hiding, laughing at the rookie.

I was transferred to Engine 29 in 1951. I was still a "trial man" with a month to go before my confirmation into being a full fledged firefighter. About a week into my stay at Engine 29, a veteran firefighter named Ziggy was telling the guys that he heard Patrick walking around the dormitory again. My first thought was that here we go again, it's prank time.

The story was that Patrick committed suicide in the officer's room on the second floor which was next to the fire fighter's dormitory where you would hear him walking around. I was laughing to myself, Yeah! Ha Ha, Ziggy! Yeah! Yeah! Another Moe story, right! Ha Ha Ha! Oh yeah! I'm going to swallow this one Ziggy! Tell me some more. According to Ziggy, Patrick's troubled soul was still earth bound on our second floor.

The strange part after this one day of story telling about Patrick, the subject was dropped for the three years I was assigned to Engine 29. I also discovered that Ziggy was honest, straight forward and conscientious, and was not into any type of foolishness.

About a year later, I was assigned the 3:00 A.M. to 7:00 A.M. watch. You had to stay awake, because you were responsible for recording all the fire calls throughout the city, plus responding to your own calls. One mistake and you were going down on charges!

I decided to go to bed early, so that I could be rested and alert on my watch. I went to bed at 10:00 P.M., and I was not sleepy at all. I was not accustomed going to sleep that early. I tossed and turned. I was disgusted with myself. I couldn't sleep. Everything was quiet downstairs, and there was no traffic noise outside. So there I was in bed, and I heard someone walking around the dormitory. There were 12 windows in that dormitory with street lights shining in, giving enough light to see anyone walking around. I sat up, but I did not see anyone. There was no one walking. But, it sounded like someone walking. The footsteps approached me, stopped, and walked away.

This engine house used coal for heat, and had radiators. The footsteps went to one of the radiators. Now, there was a little sound at it, like someone tapping it. I thought, OK, the boys were playing games. I would have thought differently if the pipes leading to the radiator were not coming from downstairs. This must be the time they are going to do the ghost story of Patrick hanging himself. Ziggy was on duty. Maybe he was not the good guy I thought him to be.

I quietly got out of bed, sneaked up to the pole hole, and looked down. The man on watch was reading a magazine. The other men were playing cards and Ziggy was among them. Everything seemed all right. I hoped I wasn't hallucinating, even though I was primed about those Moe capers. I don't want anyone pulling my leg like some gullible rookie. I silently got back into bed. Then walking resumed, again right to my bed. My thoughts were that this was a neat trick. This is a very, neat trick, a classic. I bounced out of bed, and slid down the pole. The man at the watch desk looked at me and said, "I thought you were going to sleep." I told him I got hungry, and was going to check the refrigerator for leftovers.

The guys were still playing cards. They were still involved in their game of pinochle. I went through the act of getting something to eat, and left the kitchen, tip - toeing around the engine, so that no one could hear. I took the long stairway back to the dormitory. I even walked on the side of the stair boards, so that they might not creak and give me away. It was back to bed again!

Again someone is walking the floor. I don't see anyone! Something is very peculiar here. Was there truth to that story? Ziggy is a very serious type of guy. He is not like some of the other jokers and pranksters. He's on the up and up.

I was going to do this one more time to see if anyone was pulling any angles on me. Again I sneaked down the long stairway. It had swinging doors at the bottom. I peered through. The watchman was still reading his magazine, while the others were still playing cards. I stood there for about ten minutes, when the card game broke up. I had to zip upstairs so no one would detect me. I was back in bed, but no one came upstairs. Here came the walking back to my bed. So I finally said to myself, 'OK Patrick, I believe you're here. I don't know why you're here, but I believe just like Ziggy, that you are here!"

After I made that statement, I heard no more walking or any radiator noises. No nothing! I stayed up quite a while longer, and it was peaceful and tranquil. Therefore, it could not be anyone pulling a trick on me, because it immediately stopped after I acknowledged Patrick's presence.

It could be that Patrick was still paying a penalty for committing suicide. His troubled spirit might possibly be confined to this earth at Engine 29 as a punishment.

Ernie/Figure 5

ERNIE

Back in 1989, I received a phone call from my friend, Mike. I used to tell him some of my ghost yarns at the ballroom dances we both attended. He asked me if I was still interested in getting stories about ghosts. I told him I was, but I haven't been able to collect any since I have been working on my two cook books. He said that his tenant has a story worth while looking into. It's a story concerning her 15 year old grandson who was stabbed in the neck and killed. The police have never found out who did it. He asked me if I wanted him to make an arrangement to meet his grandmother. If I did, he would give her a call to get an appointment. I said most definitely, the murder alone seems interesting enough to warrant a call.

He preconditioned her of my coming, that it wasn't concerning her grandson's murder of which she was tired of talking and being questioned, but about his ghost presence in her home. It was a few days later when I took time off from writing my cookbook to go to her home.

I was greeted warmly by an elderly black lady, asked to sit down, and asked if I wanted something to drink. I accepted some ice tea. We talked briefly about current events, weather, and then got on to the subject of her grandson, Ernie. How does he contact her or her family? What things does he do, good or bad?

She told me, he was very active in her home. That he would telephone her, and she would talk to him, or there would be a knock on the door and no one was there. I thought to myself, oh well, someone in the family is playing games with her, but I might as well appease her and continue listening to her story.

Before going on, I asked how many of Ernie's brothers were living in their two - flat, because everything she told me so far didn't sound very convincing. After telling me his two older brothers, plus two older sisters were living there. I assured myself that one or both of the brothers must be imitating Ernie's voice, or knocking on the door and running away.

Next, she related how her grandson Lucious talks to Ernie. She has heard Lucious saying to nobody, "Will you just leave me alone. Don't bother me." This started shortly after Ernie's death when Lucious was 5, and now he is 8. On other occasions he would gleefully play with Ernie or with some imaginary playmate, as we know so many youngers in this age bracket do, but she thought it was mostly only with Ernie.

On one occasion, when she got angry with Lucious and was scolding him, Ernie apparently didn't like it, because his picture came crashing down from the wall. He must have felt that Lucious should not be treated so meanly. She thought, he adores Lucious! Besides being protective of him, he would do little things for him. For example, one day he wanted to know where his ball was, and immediately his ball came rolling down the stairs from the upper flat. She claimed no one was upstairs to roll the ball down or hear him. Again I might say, that personally, I thought there must have been someone that heard, and she was not aware of them. Someone must be fooling with her. I got to ask Lucious' mother what she thought. She emphatically exclaimed, "He just isn't playing with make believe people!"

I asked grandma of other occurrences. She related to me another incident. On this particular day, when the whole family was sitting at the kitchen table debating what to have to eat, and not able to decide on one thing, Lucious started to cry because he was so hungry. The deep freeze door of the refrigerator popped open, and out came a box of frozen fish sticks, Lucious' favorite.

I also wanted to know, since Ernie talks to her, if she ever asked him who murdered him. She had, but after she did there was always deep silence. She thought that it was some close relative which he wants to protect, even though he was harmed so terribly. There would be no gain by the revealment, only more hurt, and things would not change as far as his status was concerned; he is willing to forgive.

The daughter who came downstairs in the middle of the my conversation with her grandmother, added another episode of Ernie's good deeds. It was after she and her grandmother left the doctor's office. They were going between two parked cars to reach their car which was parked across the street. Grandma was in deep thought, because the prescriptions and treatments she was getting were not making her feel any better. She stepped out without looking. A car was swiftly going in reverse toward her from out of nowhere. The daughter said that she did not see the car, because of the direction from which it was coming, and had no time to react in any way. Grandma was pushed back by some unseen force, right back into her, almost knocking her over. This act saved her life! They both felt it was Ernie's doings.

Now I changed my opinion, because everything sounded so truthful, and I felt that they had nothing to gain, so why should they lie. They had one more event to tell about. It was concerning grandma going to the doctor with the same symptoms four times, without getting any help. One of the symptoms was breathlessness, accompanied by a dry cough. At times she would also have symptoms such as fever, chills, and a headache. The doctor was treating her for influenza, with all kinds of antibiotics, and they weren't helping.

Grandma got herself a family medical guide. She was desperate and distraught, but was not the kind to give into despair. She searched and searched, hoping to find something that would give her a clue to what kind of sickness she might have. She gave up her search. She laid the opened book on a table; she was feeling just terrible, when she noticed that the pages of the book were flipping over, and then stopped. Out of curiosity, she went to the book. It was left open to the page where it explained "Farmer's Lung" disease.

Inquisitively, she read about the symptoms that matched hers, and she discovered that .this disease is caused by dried pigeon droppings. Her daughter said, "Grandma shrieked", 'Praise the Lord!' And when everyone settled down, they all agreed that Ernie was the "savior".

I asked what was the relationship between the illness and the pigeon droppings. The connection was that they bred pigeons in their garage loft. Grandma would go up there to clean the droppings or to feed the pigeons, and would apparently inhale the fine droppings, thus getting the "Farmers Lung Disease".

Grandma gave up her pigeons, and had a complete recovery. I said, "The next time I get very sick, and the doctors are not helping me, I want to borrow Ernie!"

Rita/Figure 6

RITA

Rita, a new acquaintance of mine, told me how back in 1967, she had to go to Portage, Pennsylvania to meet her father-in-law for the first time. Her story was—

My father-in-law, Giovanni, lived in an old three story wooden house with a basement and attic. When I arrived, its drab exterior gave me a chill just looking at it. It had a scary and depressive appearance. That it was also a damp and gloomy fall day did not help matters. No other building had ever affected me like this.

When I entered the house I felt a little cold. I thought maybe it's just because it was an old wooden house. Although later when I had to go upstairs for something or to the bathroom, half way up, I would get a cold chill up and down my back. It would stay with me until I got back downstairs. This went on for a quite a while.

After staying there for several days, my three month old son, Jimmy, was really fussing and crying. He was giving me quite a rough time. Since he was so tired, I decided to take him up to bed, and I would lie down with him for a while so that he would calm down and fall asleep.

It was 8:30 in the evening, and being fall, it was dark early. I took the long climb up the unlighted stairway. Again the cold feeling resumed, but I had to get Jimmy settled down. I took him upstairs even though I felt very uncomfortable there. I took him into the "boy's room". They also had a room they called the "girl's room", because there were two boys and three girls in the family, each having their own room. As the family grew they added more bedrooms.

I laid down with Jimmy in one of the three beds. Little Jimmy fell right asleep, and I shortly afterwards. All of a sudden something woke me, and as I opened my eyes, right in front of me was a lady all dressed in black with a black halo around her head. Her face wasn't clear, but I could see that she had her hair in a bun, the old fashion way, or as the Italian women wore their hair at the time.

I screamed "bloody murder". I screamed so hard that my husband ran up the stairs to see what was going on. I was trembling and hysterical with fear, all the time screaming. My husband was about to slap me, but instead he grabbed me and shook me. I snapped out of it, comforted by the fact that my husband was there. The figure disappeared as soon as he came into the room.

He asked me what happened, and I told him about awakening from a deep sleep to find a mysterious figure of a lady in front of me. I described the lady to him. He told me it was my imagination, but he knew better as I was later to find out.

When I went downstairs after this occurrence the father-in-law said, "Boy, that baby sure can cry loudly!" I was very angry with my husband Joe, because he didn't prepare me for something like this, yet knowing there were strange doings in the house. Later he told me if he did, I probably would have never come to see his parents.

This lady never left me alone. Whenever I went into the girl's room alone, I would see her behind the door. I would not go upstairs alone any longer. Even when accompanied, I would carry a rosary and pray all the time. I would not go to bed until the father-in-law went to bed or when my husband did. I would stare at the door until I fell asleep from exhaustion. I always hoped it was a dream, yet fearing that if I did have a dream the lady would appear in it.

When my husband did get honest with me, he admitted that weird things had been happening for a very long time. He told me how some things would disappear, and then return a week or a month later. When Giovanni went to the hospital, the family went to visit him. Upon returning, all the windows and doors were open, even though they knew that they were shut when they left. Odors would be emitting from the kitchen, but nothing was being cooked. When they tried to rearrange the furniture in the girl's room, the bed would vibrate until it was put back in its original place. Whoever was haunting the place did not want any changes made.

The father-in-law said that sometimes when he went upstairs the window shades would go up and down, but nobody was there, or the nailed window would be opened. Many times he would shout at the lady to go back to hell from where she came, or "Get the hell out of here, leave my family alone." For a few days it would stop and then resume.

When I met the rest of the family, they all said they had the same experiences. They acknowledged or accommodated this apparition as long as they were not harmed in any way. They did not tell anyone since they were Catholics, and the church did not believe in ghosts until January of 1997. At times when one of the boys or girls told their classmates, they were ridiculed, so they stopped telling them and lived with the situation.

The father-in-law said the house was haunted, because of the curse that was put on his wife Anna. If he had married someone else, it would never have happened. He explained that he was at the bus station when he heard quite a commotion, with loud voices, especially a man's voice. Inquisitively, he wandered over, and found two women and a man arguing. It was concerning a prearranged wedding.

One of the women was Anna, who just got off a bus and met her prospective bridegroom and his mother. The would-be bridegroom financed Anna's ocean voyage and bus fare, and also paid a dowry to her family in Italy. The man was very haughty, arrogant, and "put on airs" as if he was doing her a favor by letting her become his bride. He expected her to crawl to him in gratitude, because she was only a poor peasant girl.

She rebelled and talked back to him, which upset him more. He thought she should gush with admiration and be humble. Giovanni was listening to all this. The man became more verbally abusive, while Anna stood proud in defiance, and spewed contempt for him.

The man was ready to strike her, but Giovanni stepped in and offered to buy the prospective bride. He was looking for a woman to marry, and he was going back to Italy in the near future to find one. The abused woman in front of him was more than he expected to find there. He found Anna very attractive, and she, in turn, did likewise, so she agreed to marry him on the spot. The man was stunned, but realizing he might lose all his money, he accepted in anger.

They went to Giovanni's church where an agreement was sealed in the rectory. The man and his mother left first and stood on a street corner off the church grounds. As Anna and Giovanni approached, the mother cursed them and put a spell on Anna, on Anna's first daughter, and on her first daughter.

It was when the prospective bridegroom's mother died, that she came to haunt the house and made everyone miserable. She stayed even though Anna passed away. This continued until Gina the eldest daughter moved away, and Giovanni, at the same time, went into the hospital.

When he returned the doors and windows were all opened. Apparently, the spirit left, because there was no more haunting of the house. The family told me to visit Giovanni any time. They jokingly said, that the ghost lady went to search for Gina.

I, Rita, was no longer afraid when I visited my father-in-law. I would go upstairs, and wouldn't get any chills or feelings that someone was there. I felt free!!!

Joe or Demons?/Figure 7

JOE or DEMONS?

This is one of two stories which a retired fellow fire fighter gave to me about himself:

Joe was a guardian of Engine 57. He lived next door to the engine house for about thirty years. His home was only about twenty feet away, thus making it easy for him to observe the fire station and to protect it from intruders. He was always a friend of the fire fighters who "ran" there. We would go out at night, come back four or five hours later, and there would be a fresh pot of coffee made by him. If we had a "run" and the engine doors would be left open and someone would meander in, he would kick them out. He would make sure that nobody would help themselves to anything while we were out. It happened many times at other fire houses, especially on Saturdays, which were steak days, that the steaks would be gone when they returned; whether they were being fried at the time or in the refrigerator. He just loved hanging around the fire house. He was in his fifties, didn't have a job, and lived on some kind of government subsistence. He liked his beer. He was really a nice fellow. He would come in and tell jokes a lot of times that were not funny. He was a friend to all.

One thing about Joe, he was not afraid to work; he would even cut the engine house grass, and that was exactly what he was doing on the day he died. He died about ten to fifteen feet from where the "cot watch" bed was, where the incident happened to Preston..., Mike..., and myself.

I do believe in demons. We know that God threw one-third of the angels out of heaven, and one of them being Lucifer. So those that were thrown out eons ago are still around. They have to account for the incident that happened to me one night after Joe's death. I believe it was a demon, I don't know, time will tell in the hereafter.

The night of this incident, I took cot watch as I usually did, because I always had a difficult time sleeping at the fire house for many years. I would also take cot watch because the TV was right there, and it was something to keep me occupied, instead of tossing and turning all night in the upstairs dormitory bed waiting for the next alarm. What I do remember about it, was that I was just laying there. I was on my back, and being on my back I just happened to fall asleep. This was unusual for me because I like to sleep in the fetal position.

For those that are unfamiliar with Detroit Fire Department procedures, a man on "cot watch" can sleep on watch, but he has to be right near the watch desk. He can not sleep during the day if he is on watch, and as you know Ed, we would be startled when an alarm would come in. We would run to the phone, take information and in seconds be out the door.

This particular night I was really startled, not by an alarm, but by something that woke me and held me down, and for a 250 to 260 pound man to be on his back and something on top, and not being able to move to say the least was something. I was scared to death! I always kid that my heart was beating so hard, that a lesser man would have died! I don't know how long the incident lasted, nor do I know why it stopped. why and whatever was on my chest, and why it got off? I don't know why! It could have been about Joe the guardian spirit of Engine 57, or my belief in demons, or a bad dream. I don't know! It could all be just conjecture. The reason I am mentioning this, is because it startled me so much being attacked by something.

I am eliminating the bad dream, because at the coffee table in the morning, much to my amazement, I was not the only one to have this occurrence! It was odd that Preston..., who was once on the Detroit Police Department had mentioned that he had the same kind of experience. A week or so later I was talking to Mike…about it, because it was such a frightful episode. He said the same thing happened to him, and you know Ed, that Mike was not afraid of man or beast.

It bothered Preston so much, that he went to his grandmother. I believe she was from the hills of Tennessee. She and her people were into herbs, folk medicine and whatever, and into some of the spiritual things. I tend to believe she was a religious person, maybe of Baptist persuasion. But anyway, what came back from Preston is evidently that his grandmother was very familiar with these type of spirits.

She commented, that in order to fight the spirits you do not sleep on your back, because it is the most likely position in which you could be violated. She suggested to Preston to pass on to me to sleep in the fetal position, then I would be less likely to be attacked, and I would work my way out of it easier, which seems to be true, for when I was on my back, I could not do anything but shake.

As you see, it was not just me, but there were two other fire fighters affected. Yet none of us could come up with a positive answer. Could it be that Joe was trying to frighten me into reestablishing my religious beliefs or was the incident fortifying my belief in demons?

25

Aura/Figure 8

AURA

This is the second story that the retired fellow fire fighter gave to me:

Ed, there was a neighbor lady that would fraternize with the firefighters. She called herself the "white witch". The fire fighters would humor her about this. At that time I felt the same about her. I wasn't as strict in my beliefs then as I am now. Now, to me witches, white or black, are evil beings who are outwardly evil or some are only evil in their beliefs. This opinion came about mainly because of the story I am going to relate.

The guys and I, after our tour of duty, which was filled with a night of fires, went to a bar down the street from the engine house. We were having a few beers after a hard nights work. There were six of us and a couple of regular patrons. This neighbor or the "white witch" came in. She was going to talk to the firemen she knew. When she sat down and looked at this one fire fighter, she got up and actually ran from that table. Her actions surprised us. We wondered what was wrong with her. She went and sat down at the far end of the bar all by herself. She looked terrified and was white as a sheet. It startled me when she ran and I wondered what was happening. I went up to ask her, but before I could say anything, she said, "You know being a white witch, I see auras on people, some are good and some are bad, some have different colors. I saw a black aura over the fire fighter's head. It frightened me so that I had to get away from him. He personified evil of the worse kind which I did not expect to emit from a fire fighter. I always thought fire fighters as being an expression of goodness."

I want to interject that when I was in Bible school, I took a couple of courses, one was anthropology, the other archaeology. The teacher that held these classes was Dr. Shaw, whom I greatly admired. He was an outstanding teacher and very respected. Dr. Shaw, a Christian person would see auras too, but he would not tell us about any of the auras he saw over people which he knew in his classroom. My respect for him convinced me that there were people with this power. If someone else told me, I would be very skeptical.

In 1975, as you know Ed, there was a big controversy about this fire fighter with the black aura over his head, because he was suspected of killing his wife. It was known by everyone in the small town in which they lived, that his wife was "cheating" on him.

I will tell you that at one time this same fire fighter, after we had a few beers together, we left for another fire fighter's home to continue our drinking. There were five of us, and one thing led to another when near the end of the night he got out of control. He knocked the billiard balls off the basement pool table, knocked over the chairs, tore down the curtains ands stabbed…in the belly with a pocket knife. I had to bandage the little stab wound. Luckily it wasn't a deep puncture, but it did bleed a little, and the black aura fire fighter was responsible for it all. That tells you a little why he carries that black aura.

I might also mention that the man was a genius. He could do any type of work, blue or white collar. He was just as good with his hands as with his brains. He could do plumbing, auto collision work, electrical work, sell real estate, do tax work, and play the stock market and profit. This is why to this date, the fire fighters that knew him, still believe he was smart enough to perform the perfect crime. He was the prime suspect, but was never brought to trial, nor was anyone else. It was then determined it was a suicide as it was first suspected, and as the fire fighter claimed.

We in our little circle of fire fighter friends never accepted this decision!

Navy/Figure 9

NAVY

I received a call from a lady who purchased one of my cookbooks. I was instrumental in informing her and directing her how to get a cookbook published for the Italian-American Club, with which she was associated.

Now that their cookbook was published, she wanted to thank me and to tell me how well it was doing. She also wanted to know how my sales were progressing, which at this time were excellent.

She worked as a librarian, and suggested that I bring in my book to their gift shop. The gift shop and I could both benefit, because they sell quite a few books. Her cookbook sold real well there, and so should mine. She wanted to show her appreciation for my help as advisor for their publication. We made an appointment to put my book on display.

I delivered my books, and in an ensuing conversation she told me how happy she was to be working at the library, and on her Club's cookbook sales, and how this was a healthy diversion for her as her husband had recently passed away.

As I was about to leave, she asked me if I had any future plans of writing any more cookbooks. I told her two were enough, and I was now working on some true ghost stories. That I now have eleven tales, and hoped to get a few more. Much to my surprise, she told me she had one. If I had time she would tell it to me.

We sat down in one of the library rooms, and she recounted her funeral experiences. Her problem was trying to get her son home in time for the services and burial, for he was in the navy aboard a ship in the Pacific Ocean. This made the funeral that much more stressful, because of the uncertainty of his arriving on time.

The first thing she did was to phone the American Red Cross. She was in no way assured by them that her son would arrive on time. They told her that the navy is good about extending funeral leave privileges, however this time the distance might be a factor.

She left the matter in the hands of the Red Cross, because she had not even started on making any funeral arrangements. After doing so, she was in and out of the home the first day, but whenever she came in she would always check the answering machine for any phone calls from her overseas son. There weren't any from him, only messages from relatives, friends, and neighbors with questions about the funeral and offers of help.

She didn't set a church or burial date with the funeral director, nor did the newspaper obituary have a date. She was determined to wait until she heard from her son one way or another.

The next day, the first thing she did was to call the Red Cross again. They assured her that her son was notified by the navy, and he probably would be calling her soon. Being a skeptic, she decided not to take any chances. She decided to have the burial services on Monday instead of Saturday as the funeral director suggested. She needed her son's support in her time of grief.

She notified the undertaker of her decision, and was getting ready to go to the funeral parlor, when the phone rang. She ran to it hoping it was her son calling. When she lifted the receiver to talk, she didn't hear any voices, but she heard oriental music. She was dumfounded. Was she losing her mind, or was someone playing a cruel joke?

She went to the funeral parlor, and would talk to everyone about it. Everyone said it must be her son trying to get through to her and it was a bad connection.

When she got home again, the first thing she did was to check her calls on the answering system. She could not find any calls from her son. She was so disappointed, and felt so helpless when the phone rang. Answering it, she heard no voices, only oriental music again. Could it be her son missed a plane and went to some bar to make a call. In his chagrin, he must have gotten drunk and didn't know what he was doing. These thoughts and many others were running through her mind. She could only cry in her emptiness.

Once again, just before going to bed the phone rang. Again no voices, only oriental music. She screamed into the phone, "Please talk or leave me alone. I'm tired and upset, I need to rest." The phone got quiet. She had to take sleeping pills.

In the morning, which was now Saturday, the phone rang again. More oriental music. She just sat there with the phone to her ear, and kept listening to it for about five minutes. All the time the music just played on and on. That was the last call.

That evening her son surprised her at the funeral parlor. The first thing she said to him was, "Did you call at any time?" He said, "NO! I had to get from ship to port, check airlines and navy flights, and I had to get a loan from the Red Cross. I had to go from Manila to Honolulu to Los Angeles to Detroit, and had no time between flights." She told him about the phone calls with the oriental music.

The son said, "It had to be Dad trying to tell you that I was on the way in the only way possible for him."

She knew her son was right, for when the monthly phone bill arrived, there weren't any calling card calls listed! This eliminated the possibility of her son making calls and not admitting them. There weren't any obscure or silent type of messages, or any with oriental music on her answering machine. She therefore, was convinced, that it had to be her husband, and that he did not realize the anxieties he would create by trying to be helpful.

My Friend Sam/Figure 10

MY FRIEND SAM

This is a story of my friend Sam, who passed away as a result of having a brain tumor. Sam and I became good friends while working on the Detroit Fire Department. We were both stationed for several years on the Fire Boat, Engine 16. Sam retired early from the department because of a heart condition. After a few years of retirement, he also developed a cancerous tumor.

He had to start taking treatments for the tumor at Henry Ford Hospital. His wife, Lorraine, worked and since I was retired, I offered to take him for various examinations, for surgery to remove the brain tumor, and for radiation and chemotherapy. The surgery was unsuccessful, and he developed more tumors on his back. He passed away after suffering for quite some time.

Sam was a bargain hunter, a junk collector, and bought old homes to become rentals. He had 11 homes and a dance hall. He turned three into rentals. The rest were filled with everything imaginable, from the present to bygone years.

Sam always had good intentions of refurbishing these homes, and either reselling them at a higher price or renting them, but mostly they would always wind up as storage houses.

Many a time Sam would try to clean up his act. He would hire one of his tenants to clean out a house. Tell him to throw out anything he thought was of no value. When he did, Sam would, on his return, go out to the dumpster and retrieve the items. He saw value in every item and could not let go of them.

When Sam did pass away, Lorraine was in a conundrum of what to do. Her decision was to clean out the homes in order to sell them. It took his brother-in-law, his friend Jim and I, two years to empty them working every Saturday. In one day we would fill several dumpsters in the alley.

One day, I was baby sitting for my daughter Laura. Upon returning home, I found a message from Lorraine on my answering machine. She was at work and needed me to repair a lock on one of her tenant's doors. I called Lorraine at home that evening, to tell her I was sorry that I could not help her out; there was no answer. I called again later, and as the phone was ringing, I was absent mindedly thinking of something else. I was startled, because Sam's voice came on after quite a few rings. Although shocked, I did leave a message after Sam's announcement message.

The strange part was, that I asked Lorraine many times to set up her machine. Her reply was that she did not know how to reset it, so she kept it off. She also kept it off, because her tenants would bother her with too many trivial matters.

The next day I called her at work. I told her I left her a message on her machine after Sam came on. She said "He did? It was off." When she got home, she called me to verify that the machine was still off, but my message was still on. Now, that was a strange phenomenon!

She claimed she came from work, and checked the answering machine. She asserted, as a fact, that the machine was still off. She put it on, and to her amazement she heard me talk. She also claimed no one could have put it on since she lived alone, and only she had access to her home.

I wondered if I was going out of my mind? She told me not to fret, because she had other weird happenings around the home. She told me she does hear from Sam, but told no one, because someone might think she is losing her mind - a sort of post funeral syndrome.

She told me, one day, when she went to the basement to do her washing, a radio came on, and some disco music was being played. Again, you have to understand that Sam was a collector. His whole basement was filled from floor to ceiling, wall-to-wall with boxes of better items. The only exception was a path to his work bench, furnace, and laundry area. The basement was huge!

Lorraine kept hearing the music, but could not find the radio. She searched and searched, and finally found it in one of the boxes. She had a heck of a time finding it. It was a battery - operated radio.

Another time, she claims Sam made her basement TV come on. She had a TV there so she could do her wash as well as watch her favorite programs.

So, apparently, Sam was still with his collection as in real life unable to part from it. While at the same time playing games with Lorraine, and having his little laugh with me.

Flying Home/Figure 11

Edward Kwiatkowski

FLYING HOME

I wished all you readers could have met by buddy Hank, my dear high school pal. We both attended Chadsey High School in Detroit in the early 40s. I met him at the football team tryouts. He stood out from everyone else because he was 6'2", and weighed about 135 pounds. I would feel sorry for him, because he would take such a beating in our practices and scrimmages. They would knock him down and he would get up and ask for more. He did not make the team, so he went out for cross country. Being so skinny, it seemed that on a windy day, he would go one step forward and two back. He was like a reed in the wind.

I met up with him again at the dances in the neighborhood. We had big band music back then. The lesser known bands would come to our local "hot spots", and I'm talking about 12 to 15 musicians. He was a terrific dancer. All the young ladies would flock to him. They would cut in on him constantly. Plus, he was such a joy to be around. He was very, very likeable, outgoing with a gift of gab. He could sweet talk any girl. If you were a close friend of his, you could always get the leftovers, and the leftovers were pretty good.

We started to phone each other, meet at dances, and at various high school programs and activities. Later on we buddied up with a fellow named Chet, whose looks and build resembled Flash Gordon in the comic strips. We became known as the "Three Musketeers."

I was a couple of years older than Hank. First, I went into the service during World War II, and when I returned, he went in, and I went to college. Upon his return, he married his high school sweetheart. This broke up the "Three Musketeers" and party times.

Our relationship trailed off over the years, until he got divorced, remarried, retired and moved to Florida. He asked me to visit them whenever feasible. This was made possible, because I retired and planned to find retirement property in Florida. While searching, I stopped at his place in Clearwater. He insisted that I stay overnight, another night, and another night.

We would talk of the good old times. One of the things we would talk about, and laugh about is when we used to skip school. This was to see the big bands play at the movie theatres in downtown Detroit. You could see a movie at 10:00 AM, and the band would come on at 1:00 PM. This was like you were in "seventh heaven".

Everyone had a favorite band. Some liked Glenn Miller, some Woody Herman, some Harry James etc. We liked all of them, but when we saw Lionel Hampton, that became our favorite band. This band was on the wild side. I mean they really played wild music. The highlight of the band was their closing number called "Flying Home".

36

When they blasted out on this number, they would drive the audience into delirious excitement. They would get you screaming, hollering, and jumping in place or dancing in the aisles. The trumpets would blare, the notes would reach heaven, like Gabriel's horn! It was exhilarating, thrilling, and intoxicating! Especially when you were of high school age, and you had all that energy. We would talk about this and reminisce.

I never did buy any property in Florida, but would make a twice a year trek to see Hank and his beautiful wife, Judy. During one of these visits I was procrastinating working on finishing my cookbook. Hank would encourage me. He even rented an apartment above his apartment, so that I would do nothing but work on my book. This gesture did the trick; it enabled me to finish my cookbook. If it wasn't for him, I would still be collecting recipes.

Hank had diabetes and a drinking problem. When we were talking, he would say, "I hope nothing happens to me before I get my social security check. I want to beat the government for at least one check. They have been beating me for all these years", and he would joke about this. This was said mainly at the age of 61. When he was almost 62, when he could collect this check, he went to the social security office to see what his monthly amount would be. He wanted to know how comfortly he could live on two pension checks, but the main thing was to beat the government for at least one check. He wanted to get some of his money back.

On top of the diabetes he got cancer of the prostate. Of course, it greatly shocked everyone! Hank just kept on joking about it, especially with his doctor. He would say to him, "I don't care what you do, what kind of medicine you try on me, new, old or experimental. I want to live at least to age 62, at least to collect one social security check. You can put me on any machine you have, any experiment you might want to try, but you get me that one government check."

I told Judy on my last visit before departing, that if anything drastic should happen to Hank, to please call. I drove back on Tuesday, and arrived home Wednesday evening. When I did arrive Wednesday night there was a message from Judy on my answering machine, that Hank had passed away. I did not want to immediately drive back. I called various airlines trying to book a flight for the funeral on Saturday. I did not have any luck! Therefore, I decided to drive right back. I arrived to Homosassa Springs, Florida, where I stayed at another friend's home. Early Saturday morning I took off for the funeral parlor in Clearwater.

I was driving along and listening to the radio. Just before arriving to the funeral parlor, I decided to change stations. I hit upon one that carried the 40s and 50s music.

I located the funeral home, and as I turned into its parking lot. What should come on but "Flying Home", a rarely played tune because of it's wildness. It was as if Hank was saying, "Don't grieve, I'm okay! I'm where I want to be! I soared into heaven as if I was 'Flying Home'! I'm home! I guess I was a good guy! I'm all set! Let's be merry with 'Flying Home', like in the good old days! Don't cry, don't feel sad! We had good times, great times, and it had to end sometime!"

It was such a surprise for me to happen to hear "Flying Home", when I could have heard thousands and thousands of other tunes. This made quite an impact on me, just when I'm going to see Hank for the last time. It was inconceivable that something like this should happen. It did not seem as just a mere coincidence. It had to be some power working. The other thing I might add, is that Hank would probably want me to end this story with this crack: "I beat the government! I got that one check!"

Barney/Figure 12

BARNEY

My sister-in-law June, went to a clairvoyant in Las Vegas. This was a common practice for her for umpteen years. She received quite a bit of satisfaction from this as well as information. Before condemning her as a misguided person, let's listen to her narration of her visit as was told to me, which was very unique and surprising.

June: My father was known to be a heavy drinker. He passed away approximately seven years ago. The first thing that the clairvoyant asked me was anyone in my family a chronic drinker. My answer was, "Yes, my father." He said, "That explains the gentleman standing behind you with this bottle in his right hand with a very broad smile on his face." I'll mention this again, "in his right hand", because of its importance. My father also said to him, "With the smile and the bottle, she will know who I am."

I have to mentioned this before I get back to the clairvoyant, and that is that my father passed away in Detroit. His body was shipped to Paris, Tennessee from where he originally came. He died in 1985. He was laid out at the funeral parlor, and prior to closing the casket the family went in to view him. My father was raised a Baptist, but did not follow it's tenets. However, his brother and family did. Therefore, my father never wanted his family to know that he did not!

Before his family came in for the viewing, my brother Kenny, bought a very small bottle of whiskey - the kind tourists buy to keep as souvenirs for display. It was either Jack Daniels or Old Grand Dad, and he put it up the right sleeve of my dad's suit coat. He said he would send off his daddy to his maker in grand fashion and happy. Consequently, we were the only ones that knew this! Just my mother, sister, brother, Art and I.

Since our family was the only ones privy to Kenny's doings, you can understand my astonishment at the clairvoyant's revelations about my father. Of course, I was delighted that he found the bottle! He! He! He!

Ed: Amazing, simply amazing! Especially when he said the whiskey bottle was in your dad's right hand. Wow! Anything else?

June: Yes, yes, he said my mother who was standing behind my father was very quiet. She did not feel any need to be near me, because it was more important to be near my sister and her family, who needed her guidance. My sister was going through a traumatic divorce after being married 17 years.

My mother must have been providing her guidance or protection. The man also asked me my mother's name, because he could not get it. He said, "What is it, but wait before you tell me, let me put an initial down." He wrote down the initial R, which was correct, because my mother's name was Rose.

Ed: What else did he tell you?

June: He told me about a ruby ring that I should have gotten from my father's mother, my grandmother. She had always said, when she would pass away, I would get her ring. I never did, for at some point or another, she had forgotten that promise to me. She gave it to one of her other grandchildren. It hurt me for awhile, because I really liked this ring, and I felt I should receive it, as I was her first grandchild. In time, I got over it.

Ed: How old were you when this was promised?

June: I was eight, but I was jolted by the fact that he brought up something out of my past that I have almost completely forgotten.

Ed: Fascinating, the least! I might go to see him, but on the other hand, I don't want him exploring my deplorable past. I blush too easily! What else?

June: He told me I had two boys. He also knew one of them was having problems, the other was doing fine. This was true, my son Erik was breaking up with his girl friend, which was very upsetting to him.

Ed: Was this your first visit to a clairvoyant?

June: Oh God, no, I have been going for several years, and to several others, but the first time here in Vegas.

Ed: Was he the best?

June: Elaine in Grand Blanc, Michigan was also very good. Then there was the one right after your mother died that I visited. She was in the Flint area of Michigan. This was a long, long time ago. Ma has been gone over twenty years now, and she passed away quickly without any obvious medical problems or of anything we were aware. Ma was relatively a young woman when she died. When I went in and sat down, she told me a few things which I don't remember at this point. But, I will always remember this: the reader just stopped and said Josephine is crying. Of course, Josephine was your mother's first name, and she was crying because she said she had gone too soon. She was not ready to go! This was only a month after your mother was gone!

Ed: Getting back to Elaine what else did she tell you?

June: I went to Elaine right after my mother died. But, the minute I walked in, she immediately told me I had two boys living in Las Vegas. I would be leaving soon to visit them. Yet, I had made no plans in so doing. I had planned, upon Art's return from visiting the boys, to spend the coming Christmas holiday with my side of the family. Upon returning home, Art and the boys called. They wanted me to be with them during Christmas. I decided to be with them rather than near the terrible sadness of my mother's passing. Elaine also knew the ages of my two boys. She told me one was 32, the other 34.

Ed: When you see these people, I hope you don't give any help.

June: Not in the least. I don't give them my name, age, or marital status. If anything, I give them my first name. I don't give any phone numbers, nor any information to them. Many people will say I'm married and many other tips. I keep my mouth shut. If they tell me something I know, I don't say anything. I don't give them any information that they can use to build a story.

Ed: You were going to tell me about a card reader you went to when you were pregnant.

June: That's the first one I went to. That was in Canada, she was a gypsy. She read cards.

Ed: How did she know you were pregnant?

June: I don't know, I wasn't wearing any rings and I wasn't showing. I just found out I was in a family way. I was only two months gone. I went with a lady friend. We sat in a darkened room. She was about to pick up the cards. Suddenly, she sat back, started to rub her belly, and said, "We are pregnant, ha, ha, ha." She told me I would have two boys. That I did want five, which was true, but I would not have five, only two boys, and that would be it. She told me many things. Guess they were incidental and not the earth shaking kind. It's funny, because every one I go to never asks me, only tells me I have two boys. Elaine pin pointed my two boys in Las Vegas, when one or both could have been at home, college or elsewhere.

Ed: When do you plan to go again?

June: I'm not sure. I guess when I want to update, ha! ha! ha! To see what else is happening. I like to go once every two years to see what is going on. It's entertaining. Less than the price of a Las Vegas show!

Ed: Now you are a true believer!

June: Why not?! You just can't deny these astonishing disclosures. I don't agree when they make statement, "There will be a robbery around you or a fire", because they see someone in uniform. That is too general!

Ed: Before we conclude, anything more of interest?

June: Just a couple more things, one, he told my son Erik, he would meet a lady who would be involved in real estate, and her name would be Teresa, which was true. The other was that he would meet two women, one named Debbie, the other Wendy. As it were, there were two women in town that were trying to start a business, and their names were Debbie and Wendy. They wanted to talk to Erik for he was familiar with show business stuff in Las Vegas. They were trying to form a modeling agency.

Ed: That was truly remarkable, that he should name three people that would enter Erik's life!

Thanks June for this most interesting and thought provoking conversation. I hope we don't start a stampede to visit clairvoyants and readers.

Rose/Figure 13

ROSE

Rose was my sister-in-law's mother. She passed away November 19, 1989, on my birthday, and a day before her birthday at the age of 75. She was cremated. Her husband Barney, who also died on my birthday at the age of 75, was buried in the family cemetery in his home state of Tennessee. Rose's final request was to buried next to him.

The family held the ashes until Easter, because my sister-in-law June's brother, Kenny, could not leave his teaching job until he had his Easter vacation. June, and my brother, Art, with their two children drove in their van from Michigan to Tennessee. Kenny and his sister, Jackie, drove down separately.

The following day after arrival, they met with the paternal side of the family at their family plot to hold services. A few minutes into the services, everyone in attendance could hear loud rock-and-roll music. They all became aggravated, full of disgust and annoyed at the rudeness of someone at a time such as this, which was unmannerly behavior in a cemetery. June was most upset, and looked around to see who could be so cruel at a time like this. Here they were mourning in their sorrow, holding services, and someone stupidly put on loud rock-and-roll music.

A young family member approached June, and told her, "The music is coming from that van." She said, "What van!" He pointed at a van. She was stunned, because he pointed at her van. She said, "That is my van, I am here, and the keys to it are in my purse, the van is not running, and the radio in it has not worked for over a year." Under these circumstances anger turned to shock. Fortunately the music immediately stopped, and the minister resumed and finished in an abated breath.

Naturally, the first thing everyone did was to follow June to the van. They found it locked. Unlocking it, June started the van, and tried the radio only to find it unworkable!

Of course, you want a solution. My explanation, once again, is Rose's spirit is trying to tell us in this manner, since apparently spirits cannot talk to us directly. She was thanking June for bringing her and Barney together again. Being married for 40 years, they were once more a couple. They were rejoicing, like at a second wedding, and they wanted everybody to know that they were joined and the journey was completed! That they can now rest in peace, and this was their way of telling us.

Seance/Figure 14

SÉANCE

Before I begin my interview about a séance, I would like to quote Dr. Richard Brooks, professor of philosophy at Oakland University who said; "Mediums and spiritualists are 90 percent frauds. They presume to be able to pass along to living kin messages from dead loved ones." His remarks make me very happy, because I will be working with the 10 percent non frauds.

This interview on séances which I recorded, is with a very refined lady named Bess, whose husband was taken to Henry Ford Hospital in Detroit, examined, declared to have stomach cancer, operated on, and predicted to only have six months to live. All his internal organs, including his hip bones were infested with cancer.

I made Bess' acquaintance when I worked as a carpet salesman. She wanted to buy carpeting, but did not know how to measure the amount she might need. I went to her home, to figure out the measurements. In the ensuing conversation I was told that she was a widow twice, and both husbands died of cancer. I asked her what kind of help did she try to get? Radiation? Chemotherapy? She said cobalt, and including meeting a medium for séances.

Since I knew nothing about spiritualists, mediums or séances, I decided to interview her, and here are my results:

Ed: What was your reason for attending a séance?

Bess: At this time my man, Michael, knew he had cancer. He knew he would not live very long. He had tried all medical science available, and they could not help him. He and I were in such great despair, that we reached out towards any assistance to prolong his life, no matter how outlandish it might seem. When he was handed a card about a séance to be held, he said what do we have to lose, lets take chance on this. We had no idea what we were getting into, but it gave us hope.

Ed: So he was desperate to prolong his life.

Bess: Yes, also because he was in such excruciating pain, and we attended the best of hospitals available, and tried the best they had to offer with negative results. You must understand this was in the 1960s, and medical science was not very advanced in pain treatment.

Ed: What were your thoughts on this?

Bess: I thought it might be a fairy tale that might come true! You do not believe it, and everyone is telling you that it is not true. It was said that everything is wired, everything is fixed when you go in there.

Ed: What was your first meeting like?

Bess: We went to Henry's place. Henry was the medium. There were many other people, and we all sat in a circle. Henry sat at the head of the circle, and would go in to a trance in order for any help to take place. This is probably not the right explanation, but we can't explain it. They sang certain hymns. One in particular which was the prayer and the hymn, "Nearer my God to thee." When they sang it, Henry went into a trance. Then, trumpets would appear over certain members. They would levitate above them.

Ed: About how many people would have these trumpets above their heads?

Bess: About six, and my man was one of them.

Ed: How many people were there?

Bess: Twenty people. These trumpets were about two feet long. The kind you would see on Christmas cards that angels held. They were long and slender. The room was dark, but when they levitated, there was a ring of light. Then all of a sudden these trumpets would come to your ear. It would plant itself at your ear and talk to you. It would tell you things that were secretive, only apparent to you. Not the embarrassing kind.

Ed: Could other people hear what you were hearing?

Bess: Yes, but they would talk to one person at a time in a very muted tone. You would hear it very plainly. You could tell it was coming through the trumpet. The trumpets would come around Michael, and there were several. The trumpets would land on the parts of his body where the pain was the greatest. A voice would come through and tell him this would alleviate the pain. It was going to be better, and it was! He came out of the séance always feeling better. It was just something we just did not understand, but it was helpful, and that is what we wanted.

Ed: How often were the séances held?

Bess: Once a week.

Ed: For how many months, years?

Bess: For about a year.

Ed: Always at Henry's place?

Bess: Yes, except for one time, when it was held in our basement recreation room.

Ed: Well, this is most interesting! Where there any changes? More or less people?

Bess: No changes, same amount of people, same trumpets, same lights, same voices, and I might add, that none, none of these participants were in our basement ever before. Never!

Ed: Wow! You must be kidding! Really!

Bess: I would swear on Michael's soul if I had to!

Ed: You say, that all these sessions helped him, even though the several operations he had, all the medicines and drugs he received did not. Unbelievable! Yet, séances did!

Bess: Unbelievable, but true.

Ed: How long did this extend his life?

Bess: For about a year!

Ed: Only a year why not longer? What happened?

Bess: It was this one night, about a year later, the medium went into his usual trance. A voice came through, like from up above. It said to everyone to listen carefully. "You have been together, meeting for several months, you have taken these meetings for granted like this, but this will no longer be, this is the last night that you will be sitting together to have these phenomenal experiences. Henry will no longer be with us. He will leave you. Next week when you meet, nothing will happen. Many of you in this circle will believe that you might be chosen to head this group or to continue on, and you will try, but it will not come to pass." This is almost verbatim. Next week we met, and he was gone!

Ed: Was it announced that Henry passed away?

Bess: That's right. He got home from his office. He was going to lift the garage door to put away his car and dropped over. He had a heart attack!

Ed: After that announcement, did the meeting break up?

Bess: No, there was one gentleman that was quite active in this and he tried without any success. Henry's wife also tried. She thought she could continue his work, but as it was foretold, nobody could!

Ed: Since this happened did you try to go to séances held by other mediums?

Bess: No, the life strings were shortening, and my man got extremely helpless and bed ridden. He could only talk in a whisper. The tumor was metastasizing into his hip bones from his pancreas and through the stomach.

Ed: Therefore, he did not last long?

Bess: Not much longer. I must also include this; that after the doctors opened his stomach and looked at his pancreas, they announced he had only six months to live; he lived gallantly three years longer. Every time he would enter the hospital on crutches, and then a wheel chair, the doctors would shake their heads in disbelief. Michael was a good boxer in his younger years. He accepted his sickness as a challenge - as a bout, where he would have to go down swinging up to the last punch. He took the hits in silence and was never irritable no matter how much pain he was enduring. In order for me to continue, I had to feed off his courage. Otherwise, I would have physically and mentally broke down!

Bess/Figure 15

BESS

Bess was refined, elegant and highly intelligent. She could be compared to Marilyn Monroe as far as figures are concerned, but she was a natural redhead, rather than a blonde. She had the same sexual attraction. Bess being a widow twice, and I a divorced man, I began having designs on her.

In order to meet her again, I made a call to her on the pretext of inquiring about the workmanship of the installed carpeting. I requested that I may see the appearance of it, to see if the choice was good or not. Of course I had ulterior motives to meet her once again, to take her out, and to start dating her, because she had this strong sexual appeal.

She worked at one of the local manufacturing firms as a receptionist. She would turn all the men's heads when she walked by. They called her "the Pepsi Bounce". Her friendliness was often mistaken for flirtation. She spieled wantonness, yet she had all this grace about her. She was always an angel in church, a lady on the street and a great lover as I was to find out later. She had what one would call "class."

She was a libra. When you entered her home, everything was beautiful. Her home was very decorative, in very good taste, an interior decorator's dream - lovely curtains, furniture, pictures and decorations that just flowed with each other. Rooms would be livened with flowers from her garden.

She was from the "old school" as one would say in the '90s. She believed in complementing her man, taking two parts to make a whole marriage. Although she worked, she would rather be at home as the ideal housewife, making a beautiful setting for her husband, and having a delicious meal waiting for him. She was an outstanding cook. She dedicated herself to her man. She believed in the division of duties with the man doing work outside the home, and the woman indoors, except for gardening. She would get upset with women radio or television announcers, for she would rather listen to a man's masculine voice than a woman's. To her, women should be home bodies. So when I came into this atmosphere, it made me immediately want to be with her as soon as possible.

I asked her for a date; she consented. We dated for several months before I was invited to come into her home for dinner. This day, she met me dressed in a striking long gown. There was candle light, soft music, and cocktails, setting a most romantic mood, to which I was not accustomed. It was as if she came from a different era.

This was the beginning of what I thought would be a solid relationship, but someone or something thought differently, because of the different occurrences I started to experience. When I would go to her home, and she had to leave the room to get something from some other room, the room in which I was sitting would start getting cold, and would only normalize upon her return. If we were talking and she had to leave the room to get us a drink or to check on the meal she was preparing, and I tried to follow her in order to continue our conversation, the door of that room or any other would shut in my face. Of course I would find this odd, but I would, disinterestingly, push the door open and continue our talk. On the way back, she would go first and again the door would shut in my face.

I thought that the house was sitting unevenly or the floors were slanting or the doors were hung improperly. At this time I did not say anything about this, nor did she. The door closing continued until one day we were having a little spat about my talking to a lady at a Sear's Department Store.

An unfamiliar woman asked me where the hardware section was. Bess was not within hearing distance, an did not hear what was said. She assumed I was flirting. When we got to her home, a bit of jealousy came out. We started to quarrel, and I tried to explain my innocence; she would not listen as she was very upset, and went into the sewing room. I followed, but rather than the door shutting in my face, a large clock on the mantel of the fire place came crashing onto the floor. I was shocked because I did not touch or bump the mantel or the clock. I said, "I did not do that! I have no idea how that happened! That just happened!" Bess said, "I know you did not do that. You don't have to apologize. I want to explain something to you. Please sit down."

"Ed, I told you about my first husband Michael, the one who I tried to help by going to the séance. His presence is still here. He is the cause of these unusual doings. He said to me just before his death, that if there was any way possible to communicate from the outer world, he would do so. He said, 'You are my inspiration, my life, my only love. I believe there will be a way after I leave this world. I want you to pay attention and to listen to impressions at all times. There may be a way we do not understand. I might be able to communicate with you, or to warn you at some time or another. If someone has an ulterior motive that is not good and could harm you, I will try to give you a sign or some sort of message. I hope to get through to you. I know God will allow me to help you, because of all the hell you went through on account of my sickness.' As you see, God allowed him this privilege."

She continued, "Our argument following the Sear's incident must have made him angry. He feels you must have unfavorable designs on me." I replied, that I thought he was jealous and did not want anyone to have her, or he just did not like to see us argue, and that he must realize that my feelings towards her were not just lustful as they were in the beginning.

"Perhaps," she replied, "but nothing like this transpired when I was dating my second husband. Although, I have to tell you that something similar happened once before, and this is what I want to tell you about. If you recall, I told you how incapacitated and depreciated physically Michael got before he passed away. He was in such a bad state, that he could summon me only by ringing a small bell he had at his bedside. I put this bell away when I married my second husband. If I kept it around, you probably would have heard it, instead of the clock falling off the mantel or closing doors."

Continuing, Bess said: "It was a little after a year of Michael's passing, that my good girl friend and old school chum telephoned me. She told me, 'You can't be so withdrawn and always staying alone. You haven't gone anywhere. You haven't done anything. It is high time you get out and meet someone, and I have the perfect person for you. It's the handsome young man I introduced you to when we were shopping about five months ago. This young man would like to meet you again now that you are all alone. I am going to arrange it so that when you come to my house he will also be there. You will meet to have an evening together. Then you can decide if you want to date him or not.' I consented. We met at her home. I was quite impressed with him."

"The following day I received a call from him. Would I go out on Friday night? Would I let him see me? We would go to such - and - such a place. We made a date. On that day he came with a corsage, was dressed smartly, and we went to a wonderful show, a stage play. He was a perfect gentleman, and asked to see me again."

"We went out three or four more times. He always met me at my front door, and walked me to my door upon returning. He never came in. On our last date he insisted on coming in for he wanted to talk to me some more. We went in, and sat in the living room. He got real friendly and said, 'I want you to know you are really my type. You are the one I have been looking for all these years. I am sure this could be the match for which I have been waiting.' Just as he said that he wanted me to be his, the bell rang."

"It startled him, the bell rang so clearly. He exclaimed," 'My God, what was that?'

"What did it sound like?"

'It sounded like a bell! Who rang it? Who else is here?'

"No one!"

"Again, as soon as he got me in his clutches the bell rang. That really upset him!"

'I don't know about this place! I keep hearing bells and they are no in my head! There is something very peculiar in this house, when you don't hear anything and I do! I'll have to be excused!'

"I did hear the bell, but I would not tell him. After that I never heard from him again."

"Bess, what are you trying to tell me?" I exclaimed. Her reply was, "I believe Michael's spirit is here, or some higher power, some force we don't know about, and we don't know how to use it. But, something happened; that bell rang, because I not only heard it, but he also did. It was a definite warning to me! I was not to take seriously what he was saying to me, and not to further our relationship, that it was a fictitious reason. He had only a special personal reason of his own, but it wasn't good! I was made to feel by someone or something that it was not good for me. Later it was borne to me through a reliable source very close to him, that he did marry and the marriage dissolved into a disaster. He was a wife beater and a womanizer, who never showed love or tenderness to his wife."

Bess told me she would have continued using that bell as protection when I came along, but she put it away since it never came into use during her courtship with her second husband or during their many years of marriage, because Michael accepted her second husband.

As for myself, I must have hit the nail on the head when I said to Bess during our conversation that I thought Michael was jealous. Our relationship after that prospered. We had a continual romance for ten years without any interference from Michael. Thank God!!

The Soldier/Figure 16

SOLDIER

I attended an all-classes high school reunion picnic in the summer of 1996. I just celebrated my 50th high school class reunion in September, 1995. Our class was a large one consisting of 367 graduates. I didn't get a chance to talk to many as thoroughly as I wanted. This gave me a second chance to do so at this picnic.

As everyone realizes, there are a lot of questions by your classmates about what transpired in your past after leaving high school, especially ours since so many went directly into the armed forces during World War II.

At this picnic everyone was trying to gather this information to fill in those years of separation or for reasons of politeness or inquisitiveness, such as questions of marriage, family size, deaths, health, jobs held, retirement and future plans.

The classes with which I was familiar, included 1942, '43, '44, '45 and '46, the World War II classes. There were many questions about what branch of service one was in, and if one took advantage of the G.I. Bill, that was given to attend college free, and an additional monthly money stipend.

After many greetings and exchanging of pleasantries, we would of course seek the most familiar faces, the ones we were closest to in our classes. One classmate and his wife were not only past classmates, but also past neighbors. They asked me what I did and what was I doing presently. I told them I worked for the Detroit Fire Department for 30 years, and did substitute teaching on my days off for 21 years. Since we worked 24 hours on duty and 24 hours off, one day I would fight fires, and the next day, I would be fighting kids.

I also told them that after I retired I wanted to keep myself occupied, so for five years I taught driver education for a suburban high school. It was immediate driving on the road rather than on a course, until I got "burned out". Many students did not know their right hand from their left or vice versa. I would tell them to turn right and they would turn left, and these occurrences would be in heavy traffic. Some would stop for birds sitting on the road with a car right behind us.

After getting "burned out", I decided to move on to being a tour director on busses where I thought I would reach the height of happiness. A retiree's dream, because I would receive a small salary, rooms at the finest hotels, some complimentary meals, see the U.S. and Canada, and tips at someone else's expense. It seemed to be a choice job, but again I "burned out" in 4 years. Burn out rate was 5 years.

I found out 15 - day, 18 - day, and 21 - day trips "baby sitting" senior citizens, and trying to maintain a rigid schedule was not as glamorous as it might appear.

Since I dropped out of teaching driver education and being a tour director, I still wanted to keep busy. I decided to write cookbooks, based on fire department cooking with engine house anecdotes included. I wrote two cookbooks. They sold way beyond my expectations, which encouraged me to continue writing, only I changed subjects. This time it was to be ghost stories. When I told my former neighbors my plans, Marianne, the wife, was so overjoyed because she knew a very interesting ghost story, which she proceeded to tell me.

This was about their friend, Dan, from Dearborn Heights, Michigan, who worked with their son. Marianne related how Dan had a birthday party for his mother. There weren't any friends, just family. The birthday cake was in the kitchen and candles were lit. Dan's mother had to wait at her cake as Dan was taking pictures of her at various angles, in different poses. He took a whole roll of pictures. This party was held three years after his father's death.

When Dan brought the films home after development, and took a look at them, he was in shock! From the twelve pictures taken in the kitchen, one of them showed his father looking through the kitchen door, with just a part of him showing. He was in his World War II army uniform. He was looking only at his wife.

This was the only picture like this, because it was the only one that had the kitchen door in it. Dan showed all his relatives and friends that knew his dad, and they all verified that it was him. Marianne, who knew his dad said, "If I didn't see the picture of Dan's father, I would have said that he was crazy, but I saw the picture, and he is telling the truth!"

I questioned the fact that it was a true picture. I believed it was a double exposure. If someone would forget to advance the film to another frame and then took another picture, it would come out a double exposure. It would even happen on the old 8 MM movie cameras if a person took one side of a movie roll and then the other side. If again one forgot to take the film for development, and also forgot that the film was used previously, using that film again; it would come out a double exposure.

A friend of mine did just that. He took movies of a Memorial Day parade, and then the movies of the aftermath of the 1967 Detroit race riots. After the film development, he found the Memorial Day parade marching through the riot rubble.

Marianne passed on my thoughts to Dan, who insisted that this was not the case. The family had only a few facial pictures of his father in uniform. Those only had face, cap, and shoulders. One facial picture of him was in the living room, which could not be seen through the kitchen doorway. The picture of concern had his full body length.

Another important factor was that the picture also showed his World War II shoulder insignia patch. Dan went to an army and navy store to verify if this division patch was the same as listed on his army discharge papers. This was found out to coincide.

Dan said it would be impossible for anyone to put an image of his father, such as exists on the film with him standing and peeking through the doorway, full height, since there is no picture of that nature to have been transposed. "You have to have trust and belief in what I am saying. My Dad, three years after his death, is still looking out after my mother."

MIND OVER MATTER?

My friend Alice was watching TV, as I was preparing our evening meal. She told me the screen turned blue. I asked her what she did, and she said she did not do anything. "It will come back, it happens to my TV", she answered. We waited and waited, and it remained blue. I tried changing channels, turning the cable on and off, as well as the TV on and off. I tried my upstairs TV and it worked fine. While I was trying to figure out what was happening, I received a phone call from the cable company. They wanted to know how my cable TV was working. I told them of my problem, and was transferred to their repair department. I told them that I had cable TV installed three days ago, and now I'm only getting a blue screen. I was told to put the VCR into the TV mode. Upon doing it, the screen turned white. The operator put me on hold, apparently trying to get some help. When she returned, I told her that I don't blame the cable company for my problem, because I have had these kinds of happenings all my life. anything that I purchase or have repaired, I have to take back the second time. I have to go back twice! Or, it has to be the ghosts fooling around with me. She said, "Huh?"

I explained to her that I'm writing a book on ghosts, and they are pestering me, wanting to discourage me from continuing for some reason. I told her one of my stories, which she found very interesting. She made an appointment for a repair man to come out in a couple of days.

After talking to her, I went to shut off the cable TV, and could not! I shut off the regular TV, then tried to turn on the TV again to see if it would change things, but it would not come on! I was beyond myself! I was befuddled with all these occurrences, but life must go on!

Alice and I had our dinner, and I resumed my ghost writings. I like a good battle! While writing, my son Jon called, because my 70th birthday was coming up, and he decided to get me tickets to the stage version of West Side Story at the recently opened Detroit Opera House. It used to be known as the Broadway Capital Theatre. It was the only downtown theatre that I have never attended out of the eight large ones we had during my youth.

I told him about my TV problems, and laughingly told him it's my playful ghosts at it again. He in turn told me of his TV experience, when he was at his girl friend's uncle's house right after his funeral.

He was chatting with her brother's friend, and then there was a lull in the conversation, since they were not too acquainted, and the TV came on by itself! The remote was lying on the coffee table in front of them; no one was near the TV. They looked at each other, shrugged their shoulders nonchalantly as if it was a normal occurrence, and watched the TV in silence. In his mind he thought otherwise!

Well, I told him, "You might find this surprising, but I just cut out a small article out of the paper two days ago." I read it to him:

CAN THE MIND AFFECT
ELECTRONIC CIRCUITS?

ROCHESTER HILLS, MI-

A researcher at Princeton University will talk at 3:30 p.m. and 7:00 p.m. Monday at Oakland University about results of experiments to learn whether the human mind can have an effect on electronic circuits.

Brenda J. Dunne, manager of the Princton Engineering Anomalies Research laboratory, will give her presentation in the Gold Rooms of the Oakland Center.

I collect these type of articles because of all the skepticism there is attached to ghost stories and various unexplained miracles. Maybe, it is something else that is doing a lot of these things.

I am particularly concerned because so many of my stories have something to do with electronics. If there is truth in the article, it might make someone believe there are other forces at work other than ghosts which should be addressed, even if my stories are discredited.

Of course, my son, Jon, was relieved to hear this. It meant he was not going out of his mind, but things such as this run in the family.

Maria/Figure 18

MARIA

It was a cold, wintry night, when we (Carl and I) heard a knock on the kitchen door. I wondered who in their right mind would be out so late in such terrible weather. I peered out, and to my astonishment I saw Jane.

Jane was a "stunner" both facially and bodily. She was totally wet and holding a small hand bag. She wanted to know if she could stay a few days until she found a place to rent. My place had four bedrooms, and there was only Carl and I. Asking Carl if it was OK with him, he said "sure".

Carl, my roomer, was a Detroit fire fighter, who was as handsome as Adonis and built like a Greek god. He was divorced, and same age as Jane, but he had eyes for no woman, for he was still in love with his wife. He was a Catholic, who was divorced in the court of law, but not in the eyes of God. I was twenty years his senior.

We both loved to play Knock Rummy. During the fall, winter, and spring we would play two to three hours a day on his day off. He worked a twenty four hour shift, and then twenty four hours off. Carl had the reputation of being a top notch player on the fire department and I was average. When we played I sat at the end of the oval kitchen table with a window at my back, and he at the side. We played for one-tenth of a penny per point.

At first Carl was beating me severely. We would pay off when one would owe the other $10.00, and start all over again. I was out $20.00 to him. One day I was cooking, so I had to be closer to the stove. This put me at the other side of the table. This was the seat in which Maria died. He stayed put.

Maria and I owned this house jointly. We were to get married. This was before I discovered she was a schizophrenic, and an alcoholic. We had a tremendous love affair until her drinking problem surfaced. Since we were so much in love, I believed that old cliché, "Love conquers all". It didn't work, especially when she wasn't drinking and became paranoid. I had to deal with three personalities, alcoholic, schizophrenic and at times normal which made my life most hectic. I had to leave!

After I left, her daughter admitted that Maria was confined to a mental institution for about a year. She kept it a secret. She felt it would be too embarrassing if someone would find out. A few months later she died of cardiac arrest and a fatty liver. I then bought the other half of the house from her daughter.

While sitting in the seat in which Maria died, I started to get excellent playing hands. Being superstitious, I continued seating in this seat. I started to "beat the hell" out of Carl.

It got so bad, that one day I made the statement, "Carl you should quit, you don't have any luck!" He would not concede. I won $10.00, about four times. We raised the payoff amount to $15.00, and I continued winning. I couldn't do anything wrong. We played four times a week for several months. I won over a hundred dollars.

I felt I owed everything to this lucky seat. I never got such spectacular cards in the thirty years I played cards at the various engine houses. I felt that Maria was helping me, it wasn't normal - it had to be supernatural. I just couldn't be so brilliant after being so average all my life.

Jane stayed at my place longer than expected. She got caught up with (as many of his friends would call him) "Beautiful Carl", and being a good cook, she took over the kitchen duties. I never did enjoy cooking for myself or for just two. She also took over the house cleaning duties. She would also pamper Carl for she was looking for a new lover. She came to my place that pitiful night, because she broke up with her boy friend. Carl was to be the replacement, but he had eyes for no one. He was going to be celibate until he got back with his wife.

With the coming of Jane, my card hands became flat, and I had to struggle again to win a few games. I started to blame Jane for changing my luck. I compared it to a ship that had an all male crew and its luck would change once they had a lone female passenger. It seemed as if the bad luck was brought about by her, and I became the doomed ship.

When Carl would not pay any attention to her, she turned her desires towards me. Since I had some unfulfilled desires of my own and Carl was unwilling, I was most receptive to a new relationship. Of course, one thing led to another, and when it did, all hell broke loose.

In the card playing, I could not get one decent hand. It was unbelievable to get such bad hands; even Carl couldn't believe it. His bad hands were nothing compared to mine. I would write down the opening hand time and time again, so I wouldn't forget what cards were dealt to me, to show Carl what disastrous hands I was getting.

To give an example, in Knock Rummy, each player is dealt ten cards. The object is to get three or four of a kind of the same rank or sequences of three or more cards of the same suit. When I would get my hand, I would, invariably, get only one pair, and all the other cards would be unrelated. This would happen over and over again! It was devastating! It just "blew my mind," that even the law of averages was not working.

This was accompanied by such a chilling feeling of hate, and I didn't know what to do. Now it didn't matter in what seat I sat. I was beyond myself. I would have to take five or six draws before I could get three or something.

One might say it's only a card game, but it affected my thinking, drive and morale. It also gave me a realization that an outside force was combating me. It was a war I was losing. I quit playing!

I thought that ending the card playing would end this belligerency. It didn't, it only took a different direction. My two cars started to break down, costing me large repair bills. I had a son and daughter that I was supporting through college, and their cars started to break down. Strong winds would blow shingles off the roof. Graffiti was written on my garage with large gang symbols. My two lawn mowers would not start, and before I had time to have them repaired, my garage was burglarized. The lawnmowers and tools were stolen. It happened two more times.

I always felt that Maria was the cause of my card winnings before Jane came into the picture, and the losses after her coming. Also, the more romantic I got with Jane, the more deviltry and unusual things would happen. I came to the conclusion that it had to be the intimacy with Jane that made Maria jealous, and prompted her to react with such malice. I was in a conundrum of what to do? Life was beginning to stink! Jane and I decided to take a trip, hoping there would be a change when we returned. We would leave "Celibate Carl" with Maria.

The day we returned we were met by Carl. He was trying to put the house in order which was burglarized when he was on duty. He had just finished with the downstairs, and was just about to do the upstairs. He said the robbery was stopped in progress, because the neighbors noticed some teenagers entering the house, and called the police. They did have enough time to put the house in shambles and many valuables on the dining room table, but escaped before the police arrived. A lookout alerted the thieves when the police went to the wrong street corner house.

I went upstairs to find a loathsome scene. Everything was strewn about. Mattresses were overturned, drawers were emptied, books were knocked from their shelves and clothing scattered. The jewelry box was opened. The costume jewelry was still there, but the engagement ring I gave to Maria, and was going to give to Jane was gone.

Maria, apparently would rather see someone else have the ring than Jane. She, probably, was responsible for this occurrence, for she was angry that Jane used her home, and her bed, but she was not going to let her use her ring. Maria did not want to understand that she was gone, and I needed another partner in my life. She must have thought she had to be the only one I should love and no one else.

But, Maria was not done with us. She had the house infested with mice, while my neighbors did not have any. I set traps, and put out poison to no avail. Going to sleep was a bad adventure. You could hear them scratching and eating through the walls, running across the ceilings, squeaking, and scampering across the floors. A few times they even ran across the living room floor while we were watching television. You might find a mouse peering at you when you moved some dishes or groceries on the shelves. An exterminator got rid of some, but it seemed they came back in waves.

Jane couldn't take it any longer. She couldn't sleep. She sat with a broom in her hand to swat at any mouse that came by. She decided to leave. As soon as she left, the mice left with her. I regained my home, with Maria's permission. Jane said the house was haunted and under these conditions she would not return. Our relationship disintegrated.

Maria proved her point, won her case, and I sold the home! Present owners haven't had any problems!

Elizabeth-Kansas City/Figure 19

ELIZABETH-KANSAS CITY

I married an only child whose mother had passed away. My father-in-law Vince, had inherited an old nine room house, full of turn of the century furniture - good stuff but badly neglected.

Vince and I started to do some cleaning, painting and fixing before he sold his present home and moved into this place. He sort of camped in the downstairs bed room, and I would come over every day. I fixed him a hot meal at lunch, left his supper ready, would help him with work or would return to my home to do my chores.

The front door opened into a large reception area, with a short hallway running down the middle of the house. The hallway went past the staircase which led to the upstairs, and past a small wash room. It divided the dining room from the parlor. It led to the kitchen and a small bedroom. The dining room and the parlor had sliding doors facing each other. The sliding door of the parlor always remained open, because it was off its track. The dining room door was always left open so we could look out.

This particular day, I set lunch on the table in the dining room and we sat down, he on the long side of the table and I at the end of the table facing the door to the parlor. Just as we sat down, practically at twelve noon. I noticed a rocking chair in the parlor was in motion, rocking steadily - neither fast nor slow. Just moved back and forth - not minding us. It was the rocker Vince's father used constantly. We didn't dare move or leave, just waited for it to stop. I said, "I haven't been going into that parlor", and he said, "I haven't been in there for several days."

There was no wind, no dog or cat in the house, and this was not earthquake country. It continued to rock slowly as though someone was trying to soothe a fussy child, and about as fast as singing "Jesus loves me". We watched and talked about it in a whisper as we sat in wonderment and befuddlement. We finished our meal, and just watched for about fifty minutes, then it slowed and stopped as if someone got up and walked away.

My father-in-law died a couple of years later and my husband and I moved into the home. We lived in it for sixteen years. We had visiting children and grand children - never saw or heard anything strange. When my husband died, I lived alone in this nine room house.

I slept in the one downstairs bedroom, opposite the kitchen. I was working nights at a truck stop café. A son-in-law was in town for a few days, and he slept in one of the four bedrooms that were upstairs. I had gone to work - 10 PM to 6 AM shift. When I came home in the morning, he was up and had coffee made. I was hardly in the door when he asked if I came home during the night. I said,

"No!" "Well, someone was here!", he said. He had been awakened by some banging and rattling in the next bedroom, as if someone was moving or rummaging. There were sounds of doors opening, drawers opening and closing shut, with furniture being shoved about, not at all quietly, but not exceptionally noisy. He thought I was looking for something and was in a hurry to get back to work. So he got up and went to the bedroom door and called, "Do you need any help?" There was no answer. He took hold of the door handle to open it - absolute silence. He eased the door open a crack - looked inside. The light from the hallway and the street light outside showed the room unoccupied! It was neat and orderly, with nobody behind the door or in the closet.

I would have not opened that door, but he was a war veteran and very brave. It never happened again, and we never found out why or what did it.

I sold the house, and moved to Hartford, Kansas, to be near my daughter. The last few months I lived there, I had a dog who refused to go upstairs. I couldn't carry him up - he'd struggle to escape. My small grand children wouldn't go up either, but couldn't say why, just, "I don't like it up there."

THE GHOST

It seems there was this fellow who was
sitting in his room all alone and realized
he was the last person on earth.

As he sat there on his chair
he became aware...of being alone
and lonely in this world.

At this time he noticed the moon
was casting its rays in the room...
giving ghostly shadows on the wall.

Many many thoughts of events crossed
his mind in his darkest moment.
He realized how deeply depressed he was,
being so lonely and alone...with no hope
of becoming anyone or anything...

But he kept hoping for something to
happen...as the darkness of the night
settled in and the dancing shadows on
the wall began doing their routine...
all the while beaming.

More and more depressed, and it was in
one of these moods as he was sitting...

There was a knock on the door!!!!

Floyd Keeton
Red Oak, Iowa

Keno/Figure 21

Same lady wins both

Second $250,000 keno ticket at Peppermill

How was this done?

According to SHOWTIME, Las Vegas, Nevada, October 5, 1990.

Easy! A woman won this with the help of her dead father. This is no joke!

This all happened at the Peppermill Hotel-Casino in Reno, Nevada. The first time the woman won was on September 3, 1990. It was a $5.00, 9-spot keno ticket, winning for her the first $250,000. The odds of someone doing this is one to several 100 millions!

Then the unbelievable happened again at the same Peppermill Hotel-Casino on the morning of September 25, 1990, just three weeks later. Lightening struck twice...now the Peppermill is the home of the only two $250,000 tickets paid in northern Nevada. And, what was even more unimaginable is that both tickets totaling $500,000 were hit by the same 47-year-old Reno area resident, and home health care center owner.

Skeptics may scoff, but it's hard to argue with two $250,000 jackpots in three weeks, and that it was due to the assistance of her dead father. To transcend such insurmountable odds, one would have to have help from some unearthly source!

The Reno, Nevada lady said, her incredible luck was based on advice from her father who died in 1975. He inspired her to play keno at the Peppermill. She gives him credit for both wins. "It felt like a blessing from heaven. I still can't believe it."

Before the Labor Day win she was very upset, because she was not doing well in her health care business. One night in August, her father stood at the foot of her bed. He came to her in a vision, and was comforting her about the money problems plaguing her.

"Baby" She recalls him telling her, "Stop worrying, everything's going to be OK, don't worry." The message prompted her to review his obituary which contained the winning numbers.

For the second win, which was on September 25, she picked the winning numbers by looking up her father's name, Cornelius, in the game book "Three

Wise Men", and used combinations from the numbers that symbolized his name. It was her tactics that beat the odds by a milestone.

She still plays keno at the Peppermill almost every day, because she loves the "class" and style of Peppermill, as well as the friendly people. She still tells everyone, that she's sure her father is always watching over her. "My father is still taking care of me. He is smiling down on his baby. It's happening right now!"

She doesn't expect any more help for it was a wonderful gift. One could not, ungreedingly, expect more!

If you want to beat the impossible, you had better have had a great parent!!!

The Inebriated Ghost/Figure 22

THE INEBRIATED GHOST

There was a bar in the "old" neighborhood on the near west side of Detroit, which a deceased patron named Jake, haunted. Many people pooh-poohed this, saying it could be the power of suggestion influenced by a few drinks - a bar joke- a drunken man's concept on how to feel important that he should have the ability to see a ghost while others couldn't. Some supported the story, because of their friendly relationship with Jake, even though they never saw his ghost.

Jake was a "clean up" man and customer at the bar for many years. He was an elderly man in his sixties. He also lived above the bar. He was in the bar from opening to closing; he hardly ever saw the light of day. He was the pillar in the clique of the elderly who hung around the bar. He was comical, humorous and witty, with an eye for the ladies. He was the best joke teller around. He was also a favorite, because of his generosity, buying drinks for the "old timers" when they were "busted" just before pay day.

Many a time he would say that he's never going to leave the place, even after death. He said, "You will see that if something happens to me; I'm going to get back here." He would joke about how he will come back to see how the guys were behaving, and to make sure that everyone gets home on time to have supper, so they wouldn't get in trouble with their wives. He continued his lecture, telling them, "You guys can't take care of yourselves. Without me, you would all be divorced or in the 'dog house'. You'll be lucky to have me around." Of course this was a big joke to everyone, and they would chide him with remarks such as, "You can't even take care of yourself, let alone us. If you didn't live above the bar, you would never get home. Besides no one will want an 'old grouch' like you around!"

The bar was in a very old building, probably built during World War I. It was a two-flat with two rental apartments above the bar. It was so old, that at one time it had an outhouse. An open stairway led to the upper porch and back apartment. Later the back stairway and porch were enclosed, where a bathroom was added to the upper back flat, and a rest room to the bar.

The only access to Jake's front apartment was a very narrow and steep stairway at the side of the building which Jake had to use. It was almost like a closed-in spiral staircase. Any large furniture had to be taken through the back flat to Jake's place.

It was arduous for Jake to climb these stairs because of his age, and more so when he was inebriated, which was quite often. As he aged, he got to know when to stop drinking in order make those stairs. However, there were times when he slipped below the stopping line. When he did, he developed a technique, where he would take two fast steps and sit down. He kept repeating this process; take two stairs and then onto his butt, two more and onto his butt. Sometimes it was butt, butt, butt. He didn't dare stand until he got to the hallway leading to his flat.

There were times when his drinking buddies would try to help him. When he refused their help, telling them he had pride and was quite capable of doing it by himself; they would laugh at him and take him under each arm, insisting on helping him. But, in this case, architecture got in the way of good deeds. They would have to give up, because the stairwell was too narrow for three to go up side-by-side, especially if they also were a little "pie-eyed". There would be bumping, falling and cursing, causing so much noise that it would awaken and anger the other tenant. Her cure for all this would be a bucket of cold water, with a footnote like, "If you like to drink, drink this!" After this happened a few times, the "good Samaritans" let him get to the upstairs in his own particular and gradual way.

He was hired to clean the bar since he lived above it, which made him readily available to do the cleaning after bar closing, or in the morning before it opened. He would clean the tables, chairs, rest rooms, wash left over glasses and floors. But, his most important job was to keep the long mirror behind the "back bar" clean.

In the old days you would rarely find a bar without a lengthy mirror. The psychology of the mirrors at the bars was that a patron would never get lonesome, especially after a few drinks. He could look at himself, and keep himself occupied. Many would sit looking at the mirror and talk to themselves. They would be mesmerized by their own images. Often you could observe someone raising a glass of beer and saluting themselves while looking in the mirror. The only other entertainment was the radio, checkers or a game of pinochle. The bar catered just to the local people of the neighborhood. There wasn't any "outside traffic".

One morning when the owner came in, he found Jake lying on the floor, covered with bags of potato chips and pretzels. The owner got very angry, thinking Jake passed out from drinking too much. He was saying to the still Jake, "This is gratitude for free drinks, the cleaning job that gave you extra money above your pension money, and what do you do but get 'smashed' and pass out. Now I will have to get you up that stairway or have someone else do it, if possible. Those dam stairs!" He was very disgusted, but he decided to let him just lie there until he got up. He was also hoping that when he opened up, some young guy would show up, and he would pay him a few dollars to carry Jake up, or at least put him in some corner to sleep it off.

He kept mumbling to himself while working around Jake. About an hour later, he went up to Jake, and told him to get up, because he wanted to get to the cooler and Jake was in the way. He shouted at him to get up, but got no response.

Since Jake was lying face down, he turned him over. When he did this, he noticed that his lips had turned blue. It was obvious now that Jake had died, but he felt his pulse hoping he was wrong. It was a useless gesture.

Jake didn't have a family; the bar people were his family. There was a small insurance policy, just enough to cover funeral costs. There was a collection for flowers and a Mass. The body was laid out in his apartment to reduce costs. It was still in the 1930s when they did this type of display. Six of his bar buddies were picked as pall bearers.

The bar was closed on the day of the funeral, except for those that were going to attend the funeral. The pall bearers were drinking during the wake, and now were having a few before the priest arrived. When it was time to go upstairs, a couple of them had a little difficulty making the climb upstairs. The priest and two altar boys came to the home, said prayers and left for the church to prepare for Mass. They had to wait at the church for a while, because of the unexpected about to happen.

After the casket was closed, and the mourners left for church or for their homes, the pall bearers took the casket, and began their descent down the steep and narrow stairwell. Weakened because of their age and drinking, they had difficulty carrying it. They also could not carry it three to a side, because the staircase was too narrow. Therefore, two got in front and two in back. When they got to the curve at the landing, they had to raise the casket upright, putting all the weight on the two bottom men, who were cussing at the two above to bear some of the weight. Of course, the two top men couldn't, because they were raising the casket on it's end.

The two bottom men had no one to help, as everyone was in their cars, or on the sidewalk. They dropped the casket. The top popped open as it hit the stairs, and the upper part of Jake's body came out. More shouting and cursing emitted from the pall bearers. Finally after quite a struggle, they pushed the body back into the casket. They got it around the bend and slid the casket down the remaining stairs. The pall bearers once again gathered around the casket; carried it to the hearse without any further incidences, and the funeral finished normally.

When the casket-bearers returned to the bar after the funeral, they all said that falling out of the casket was Jake's fault, because he said he would never leave the place, and that was his first attempt to stay.

It wasn't long after the funeral that Jake was seen sitting at the bar with a smug look on his face, first by the owner, who tried to keep it a secret. He didn't want any one to think he was hallucinating, or trying to cash in on some publicity for the bar. He'd rather just keep it a quiet neighborhood café. This was impossible, because friends of Jake started to see him. Some saw him cleaning the place, others mostly saw him drinking.

All the bar clientele tried to get the owner to take advantage of Jake's off-and-on ghostly appearance. They wanted him to notify the newspapers to exploit these occurrences. The owners said he was concerned about the neighbors and their peace and quiet, because there was only on-the-street parking near the bar. It might also attract hecklers and if the newly acquired customers did not see Jake, they might get rowdy or verbally offensive.

A few months later, the owners felt that he was right, because Jake would never appear when there was a stranger about, but he did play practical jokes. If a new customer happened to go to the rest room, on his return he would find some of his beer taken out of his glass. It would result in an accusation that the barmaid, owner or another patron drank some of his beer. There would be an ensuing argument between him and whoever was in the bar at the time, and when they tried to tell him Jake did it, the newcomer would storm out of the bar calling them a bunch of idiots.

Jake would appear as soon as the person left, looking self satisfied, inebriated, and standing on his head. This would bring a cheer, applause, and whistles. They would invite Jake to take a drink out of their glass, but he never did.

What he did do, was to make moves or jumps for those who were playing checkers, pull the right card out of a player's hand during a pinochle game, or give a cold touch to the back of the neck of a friend for whom it was time to go home for lunch or supper. He was doing what he claimed he would do.

The only time Jake was seen outside of the bar was reported by a barmaid, who was asked by the owner to clean and paint Jake's apartment before selling the building. She told everyone that as she started to paint, she felt vibrations, and saw an unclear vision of a man. She became frantic, it scared her so, but she was able to address the apparition. She said, "Whoever you are, please leave me alone! If you leave me alone, I will leave you alone! I am going to clean and paint your flat. I will make it look beautiful for you!" She got to finish cleaning and painting the flat without any further disturbance.

The building and bar were sold. The new owner was not told about Jake, as the present owner did not want to jeopardize his sale.

Jake did not appear to the new owner for quite a while, but he did notice that no one would sit on this one particular bar stool, even when the bar was full. The customers would go to a table instead. It was explained that it was Jake's favorite seat, and they left it for him. They tried to tell him that Jake still haunts the bar, but he ignored their tales, since nothing unusual happened.

Finally, Jake was sighted by a cute barmaid. Jake, who was known to avoid strangers could not resist trying to meet the svelte and attractive "gal". The barmaid heard the door open, and felt a strong breeze waft by. Next, she felt something cold on her neck, and she whirled around. She saw no one, but it happened again. She called the owner, and told him to come right over for she was quitting, because of the weird episode.

As the factories started to close or move from the area, the clientele kept decreasing. Some, transferred to the new factory locations, while others started to move to the suburbs. The ownership of the bar and building kept changing, and less and less was seen of Jake.

Eventually, the building and bar fell into the hands of the City of Detroit, because of non-payment of taxes. The building was boarded up, and now stands empty.

When I pass the old shut-down building, I wonder how lonely Jake must be with no pretty barmaids to make passes at, and no jokes to play on anyone, unless some of his old cronies have joined him in the hereafter.

Old Lady and Her Dogs/Figure 23

OLD LADY AND HER DOGS

I had to have my rear brakes replaced on my car. I went to have them done by John, my young mechanic friend, who knew that I wrote two cook books. He asked me how I went about getting my books published, because his mother wrote a romance novel, and her submissions to publishers were getting rejections.

I told him it was no easy matter to get published. You have to keep trying and not get disappointed. Rejections are part of the game. You have to research what type of book material publishers want, say some prayers, or get lucky. I also told him I was getting rejections on my ghost story book. One of the rejectors said I had too few words. I had 23,000, and they wanted at least 25,000 words, and because of this I was at a standstill. I don't know what I will do, having come so close, yet unable to come up with more stories for it's not easy finding true ghost stories.

He said, he knew a ghost story that might help me. I asked him if it was a true one, and he answered, "Yes!" I was elated. This is what I call luck, because one long story or two short stories would give me the word count I needed. I also inquired why he didn't tell me sooner, since he knew I was doing a book about ghosts. "Because it is too gruesome!" was his reply.

He handed me a pencil and some notebook paper. He began by telling me how his brother bought a very old dilapidated house, even though he knew a distasteful thing happened in it. He bought it very cheaply, and felt that he was handy enough to bring it back to its old elegance. It had a large yard for his three children and dog to play in.

But, it was only a few months later that he told John, that he had to sell the home or his wife would leave him. She couldn't stand living in it any longer, because too many weird and frightening things were happening, especially to the children, usually, when he was working or when she went outside and left the children alone for a few minutes. They complained that they heard dogs barking viciously at them. She would hear sounds as if dogs were eating, and as if someone was falling down the stairs. The bedrooms and bathroom were upstairs. Their dog was often found barking at a spot near the bottom of those same stairs. Sometimes, he also heard noises in the middle of the night as if someone was falling down the stairs, then he would hear growling as if two dogs were fighting over something. He would go to the children's room and he would find their dog sleeping peacefully at their bed.

John didn't care what was happening in the house, because he decided to buy the home and use it as a rental. He needed it as another source of income, and the house was a bargain. He was going to school to become an engineer, and his mechanic job wasn't providing enough money.

He got himself a young female tenant who was on welfare, and had two grade school children. She was ecstatic about getting the place, because it was so difficult for a welfare mother to find any rental, especially since it was only two blocks away from a grade school.

For a while everything was fine. There weren't any complaints, but suddenly things changed. The children started to hear dogs snarling at them when they were to go upstairs to the bathroom. Their cat with it's hair on it's back standing upright, would hiss occasionally at the spot near the bottom of the stairs. She would hear the same sounds as John's brother's family did, except she would hear a loud scream accompanying the falling down the stairs. She too had to move.

John made a phone call to his brother to clarify why no one wanted to keep living in the house. His brother was surprised, he thought he made it clear what was taking place. John said he knew what was occurring, but not why. "Well I guess maybe I didn't tell you why, but everyone in the neighborhood knew why, plus the tragedy was in all the papers. Where have you been? Didn't you know about the old lady that lived all alone in that house, except for her two dogs?"

He proceeded to tell the crushing story, which went this way: The lady was in her eighties, and was living off a meager social security check. She only had one distance relative, that never kept in touch. Her only outside contacts were with a few church people, and didn't even have a phone.

A few years before she died, she made an agreement with her church, which was only a block away, that if they helped her, she would donate her home upon her death. There was always a need for someone to help her with leaking faucets, and other minor repairs. Her biggest need was transportation to and from the super markets, for she was too weak to carry anything for any great distance. The house was old and unpainted, but it was still worth about $20,000, and needed care.

The pastor agreed to help her as much as he could, but he himself wasn't getting the volunteers he needed to carry out all the repairs. The pastor said he didn't realize her predicament, and even without the house donation he would have helped her.

At the beginning, the parishioners were very concerned, and helped her quite a bit. They took her shopping, made simple house repairs, but as time went on, interest, enthusiasm and concern faded. The old lady found herself all alone again. Her only friends and companions were her two dogs, a large chow and a small terrier.

Her house was on a corner lot, bordering a wide main avenue and a regular neighborhood street, which led to a nearby grade school. It had a large fenced in yard that ran the length of the house and its rear.

Children crossing the main avenue had to go by her home in order to reach their school. They had to be helped by a crossing guard. Most of the children walked on the other side of the street from the house in order to avoid the dogs when they were in the yard. But there were always some who derived pleasure from teasing the dogs, and would throw stones and sticks at them. The little dog would yap away, the Chow would charge the fence and try to jump over it. The dogs would even go after a quiet child because of the behavior of the bullies and pests. The old lady would complain to the crossing guard, and the guard would promise to report the students, but nothing seemed to change much.

One day the crossing guard took note that the dogs had not been out for several days, nor were there any sounds or sign of life emitting from the house. She started to wonder if something was wrong or if possibly, the old lady had moved.

It was winter, and there was snow on the ground. The guard still didn't see any activity. There weren't any tracks leading to or from the house. The mail box at the gate was full. She decided to go to the house to check to see if she was unduly concerned. As she climbed the steps of the side porch, she could hear the dogs barking frantically. Once on the porch the dogs started to growl, and began jumping at the door. She got frightened. she didn't try opening the door in fear that they would come after her. There were no human voices trying to quiet them. She did knock, but no one answered. It seemed that the dogs just got more wild in their behavior.

She left, and decided to wait one more day, because it was the first day of snow, and the dogs might be let out later. The next day since she did not see any prints, she decided to call the police.

After calling, two policemen arrived. She explained to them that she hasn't seen the dogs out, nor any prints in the snow for two days. She thought possibly that the old lady moved away, until she went to the door, discovering the dogs still in the house.

The officers went to the door, and no one answered. They tried the door. It opened. They only opened it a crack, because of the dogs. Not wanting to get bitten or having to shoot the dogs, they called the Dog Pound for assistance.

The dog catchers arrived about 20 minutes later. They swiftly opened the door, charged in, and quickly captured the dogs in their nets. The policemen, cautiously, entered. It was dark in the house, because the old lady always kept her shades down. With their flashlights they saw a body on the floor at the foot of the landing. They put on the house lights, and discovered that it was the old lady with some of her body parts eaten away. She had apparently died after falling down the stairs. Of course, they put the dogs to sleep.

"So," John said to his brother. "What you are saying, is that it is not livable, because the old lady and her dogs are haunting the house." "Yes, that's what I'm saying", answered his brother.

John pondered the problem, of how was he going to keep any tenants under these conditions. He figured out, that if he got a male tenant without children, it might do the trick. The dogs hated children, and maybe the dogs' ghosts would behave if no children were present.

John got himself a male tenant. He didn't tell him anything about the haunting. A month later when John went to collect the rent, he inquired how he liked the place, and if anything strange was happening. The renter said everything was just fine. John then confessed that the house was haunted when he previously rented the place.

The tenant said that no one is going to haunt the place while he is the renter, because he is an S and S man. "What is an S and S man?" asked John. "It means I smoke cigars all day, and snore all night, and no one, living or dead, can put up with that."

House on Vinewood Street/Figure 24

HOUSE ON VINEWOOD STREET

Two brothers moved into a stately house on the Southwest side of Detroit, near the Detroit River, which is a thoroughfare for freighters from around the world. It was a two-flat, an apartment or household whereby one residence is upstairs from the other. In other parts of the country it is called a duplex.

The homes are very imposing in this neighborhood. Most of the homes were built in the early 1900's. Almost all of them were two-flats, and many had the widow's walk or widow's watch type of architecture, since these homes were near the river. The corner of the house facing the river had the appearance of a turret. It would be higher than the building itself, having three to four windows facing the river. It was used to observe the approaching or docking vessels. Ship captains would have these types of homes built, so that their wives could either wave to them as their ship passed or know when to run down to the dock to greet them. The wives would not see their husband for long periods of time, therefore, they were jokingly referred to as widows.

The older brother, Jesse, moved into the lower flat, and the younger brother, Martin, moved into the upper flat. A huge fireplace was located downstairs. a long stairway led to the upstairs. The home must have been a single dwelling at one time, and then later divided.

Soon after they moved in, the brothers started to experience strange happenings while their wives didn't seem to notice anything unusual. The front door would open and then slam shut. The brothers would hear someone run up the stairs, stop at the top of the stairs, and pant heavily. Martin felt as if someone came in, and went to the widow's watch. Martin's and his wife's bedroom was right at the top of these stairs.

Since only the brothers heard all this, their wives believed they were imagining things, drinking or making up things to frighten them. Until one night Jesse awoke his wife to listen to the noises. What they both heard were sounds as if a toddler was whimpering or softly crying. They both jumped out of bed, turned on the lights, and ran to the other bedroom to check on their little boy who was in that age bracket. They found him sound asleep.

On another occasion, Jesse and his wife, heard a woman screaming at night. It seemed to be coming from Martin's flat. They both figured Martin was having a spat with his wife. When they confronted him, he denied it, and accused them both of dreaming.

Martin had his own startling experience. He was returning home after working his factory afternoon shift. He noticed a man between the houses. The man turned and ran. Martin shouted for him to stop. The man just continued to run. He chased him, and threw a bayonet which he carried for protection when he came home so late at night. It just went through him. The unusual thing about this man was that he was all in black, with a top hat, cape over a tuxedo, and cane as if he came from a bygone age when wealthy men wore these type of garments when going to the theater, opera, or high society social.

The brothers decided to question the landlord and their neighbors. The landlord was reluctant to give out any information, but an elderly male neighbor who lived there from childhood told them that his parents used to talk about a woman who lived with a ship captain in the home. The husband was believed to have abandoned her. She could not get herself to believe this, only continued to believe that something happened to him, and that he would return. She would stay in the widow's watch constantly. Shortly afterwards she died. Everyone believed it was from a broken heart. Previous tenants would hear her running up to the watch when ever they heard a passing freighter's whistle, and sobbing when the ship continued down the river.

To the brothers this accounted for the door slammings, the running up the stairs, the panting and the soft sobbing. But, they were also concerned about the stylishly dressed man that Martin came upon between the houses.

The neighbor proceeded to tell them that as a child he saw the suave dapper man many times and his week-end parties, their merriment and gayety with elegant and sophisticated couples attending the lavish parties. He had owned a large amount of property in the area. He was constantly entertaining former and future prospective buyers. He held high stake card games after the festivities for he was a known notorious gambler.

His parents also said, that it was rumored that the gambler had hid an enormous amount of money from his card playing winnings and land sales, but the parade of tenants that occupied the home never said anything about discovering any money. Possibly, because no one ever questioned his parents or him about the strange doings at the home, and never knew about the possibility of any money being hidden. So there could be some gold or silver very cleverly concealed, and maybe the gentleman returns to check on his hoard. He told the brothers that the property owner met his demise when he came home after selling something for gold or cash. He was murdered, and the money/gold was never found.

The two brothers immediately went to their oldest brother Enrique, and told him about the possible good fortune, how the neighbor explained about the two ghosts that were haunting the home. He told them that they were both crazy, but inwardly, he thought they might be right. But, because they insisted that there might be some kind of treasure, he decided to join the search.

When they started to look for possible hiding places, they noticed a loose brick in one of the walls in the basement, and pulled out the brick. They found an old skeleton key, a little larger than the normal sized closet skeleton key. Enrique tried to pick it up, but it was too hot to hold. It was also too hot for the other brothers to hold. They said they would go through the house to see if they could find a place for it to fit, but could not. They continued to search for hiding places.

They thought about the huge fire place in Jesse's living room, that had not been used by him or the previous tenants what appeared to be a long time. There was nothing on the outside of the fire place that looked suspicious. They decided to look on the inside.

Jesse was the first to try but he was too portly to squeeze inside. Enrique was so eager to try, that they allowed him to try next. He did not have any more success than Jesse. Martin with a smile on his face, thought he should have been the first to try, because he was so thin. He managed to get up into the fireplace. He was not in there but for a few seconds when he came right back down. He had a blank look on his face, walked past everyone without saying a word. He walked out the front door and disappeared for two days.

When he returned he could not remember where he had been. His personality changed for the worse, and to this day he is not the same person he was before going into that fireplace. Enrique and Jesse believed he must have seen the devil in his hiding place, and the key must have belonged to him. Later they cemented that skeleton key into the wall.

Shortly afterwards Enrique and his wife went on a two week vacation. When they came back from the vacation, they found both families had moved out of their place, and were staying with them until they found somewhere else to go, because things got so bad at the Vinewood house.

MILLY

By Mary Kwiatkowski

My family has always placed some measure of significance in their dreams. Consequently, I've fallen into this same pattern. I believe some of our dreams are signs of things to come and sometimes they are a rehearsal for the dramatic moments in our lives so that when the ultimate tragedy finally comes, we will be able to withstand the pain. I truly believe that when we have a strong emotional and mental bond with someone we love, that a higher power sends us warning signs and practice sessions at withstanding grief. This story is my account of some very significant dreams.

Shortly after we make our appearance in the drama called life, we become aware of our fellow "players." Some of these players are merely walk-ons, some are bit players, and, then there are those who have major roles in this drama. Such was the case with Milly, my elder sister, who was just two years my senior. she was a major role player.

It is true we had fights and an occasional spat, but, by the time we approached our early teens, we had established a very strong bond. Milly was the consummate housekeeper and "little mother"; she was always looking out for me as the next two paragraphs will bear out.

We lived seven miles from the nearsest store and our family didn't own a car. We had to rely on my uncle or neighbors for transportation to do our shopping which was always on Saturday. So...when we ran out of something, we either improvised, borrowed, or did without. When I had no more writing paper for school work, Milly would completely erase one of her old math papers and say, "There, use this." One day in particular stands out in my mind:

When we left for school in the morning we had a nice westerly wind and the weather was very pleasant. As we headed for home, we noticed a shift in the wind, from west to east, that was blowing in form Lake Huron, MI., and it was bitterly cold! None of us was dressed properly for this kind of weather. As was the custom for all girls our age, we wore long, thick cotton stockings that were held up by rubber garters. To make matters worse, one of my garters broke and my stocking was flopping around my ankle. I was so cold! My teeth began to chatter and I started to cry convulsively. Milly took off one of her garters, gave it to me, and helped me pull up my stocking. My father was worried because of the weather change, and, as soon as he could see us, he came to meet us, gathered me in his arms, and carried me home. My mother peeled off my shoes and stockings and set my feet in tepid water.

As we approached our middle to late teen years, the bond between Milly and me became even stronger. When sisters spend a lot of time together as we did on our long walks (ten miles) into this little town, called Au Gres, there was much time for bonding. We would go to the town to visit friends or take part in holiday festivities. While walking, we passed the time talking (sometimes sharing secrets), singing (we harmonized), and sometimes we just walked in silence with our arms around each others shoulders. By now, we were aware that we were "best friends."

Of course, as we grew older, we had to separate because of school, work, and our respective marriages, but we always maintained our special bond and kept in touch through letters, telephone, and an occasional visit to each others home. The long distance between our cities did not permit more. Oh, how nice it would have been to live in the same town!

In my first dream, Milly was sobbing and was filled with such unhappiness that she couldn't speak. All I could do was ask questions and wait for an answer that she would give with the shake of her head. I asked her what was wrong. No answer. I asked if she and Dick, her husband, had a fight. She designated, "No!" I asked if their love for each other was still intact; she nodded. "Yes!" I asked if she and Dick were going to be separated. Again, she nodded an emphatic, "Yes!" Then, I woke up, feeling very troubled.

My second dream began with me standing in my clothes closet. I was pushing clothes down the rod searching for something; I don't know what I was looking for, but, all of a sudden, my eyes fell on this black dress. It was the dress Milly had loaned me to wear to my uncle's funeral. I screamed. "What is that dress doing in my closet? I returned it to Milly a long time ago!" The real reason for my emotional outburst was because I felt that by this dress suddenly reappearing in my closet, something terrible was about to happen. I awoke, and, as before in my first dream, I was extremely upset.

The setting of my third dream took place in Milly's kitchen in Jackson, Michigan. Milly was nowhere to be seen. "Where could she be?" I pondered. The kitchen was one of Milly's most frequented rooms. she was the only person that prepared meals. As I was puzzling over this, my brother-in-law walked into the kitchen and said, "Good morning, Mick." Then he walked over to the stove and pulled out a heavy iron skillet, took a slab of bacon out of the refrigerator, sliced it, and then put it in the skillet which he placed on the burner to fry. My! Was I puzzled. Dick never cooked. Never! I awoke and contemplated about what meaning could be derived from this.

About six months later, Milly died from infectious hepatitis. Then, the dreams came tumbling out of my memory bank and, finally, I could attach some meaning to them.

In my first dream, I was musing about the fact that Milly and Dick were still very much in love. To be separated from each other would be unbearable. This dream was to warn me of their separation by death - Milly's death.

After my second dream, I thought this was an omen of my father's impending death. He was 84 years old at the time, and so it seemed reasonable to interpret the dream this way, but, I was wrong. It was my dear sister Milly who was laid out in a black dress.

Finally, the last dream was an outright prophecy of things to come. We received news of Milly's death on a Monday morning. My husband, Ed, drove me to Jackson to be with Milly's family in their hour of sadness. Milly and Dick had three children, ages 12 to 17, and I wanted to be there with them at this time. After the first night's sleep, I went downstairs to the kitchen. I sat there by myself for a few minutes before Dick walked in. He said, "Good morning, Mick" and then we embraced and cried. Next, Dick went through the very same motions that had occurred in the third dream right down to the smallest detail. He took a heavy skillet from underneath the oven, put it on the stove and then placed into it the bacon he had just sliced from the slab.

I had two more dreams about Milly, but these dreams were in the same time frame surrounded by her impending death. My husband and I were going to visit her at the Ann Arbor, Michigan hospital, and, from having seen her a few days prior to this, I was an emotional basket case. Milly was in a coma and I had very little hope of her ever recovering. The night before we had left for our trip, I had a dream that we were ascending in the elevator and, as we rounded the corner to go down the hall, Dick was at the end of it wearing a surgical gown, mask, and gloves. All I could see were his eyes. When I looked at his eyes, I knew that Milly was worse and was not going to get through this. The next day I had such a lump in my throat, and the closer we got to Ann Arbor, the heavier my heart felt. Then, just as in the dream, we stepped off the elevator, rounded the corner, and saw Dick at the end of the hall with the protective clothing that I previously described. All I could see were his eyes, and then I knew that the end was near.

After we came home from the hospital, I was like a limp dishrag. The sadness was unbearable and I knew I was losing my best friend. That night I had one last dream. I fell asleep, but awoke in a very agitated state. I was not dreaming yet. I was crying before I even awoke, and I knew, because of the pain I felt, that these were Milly's final hours. I cried for quite awhile and then fell asleep form emotional exhaustion. I dreamed that I was in the hospital in the operating room with Milly, the doctor, and a nurse. The doctor told me that I was going to assist with the surgery to give Milly a massive transfusion. He cut a small incision in the crease by her buttocks and a little bit of something was protruding. the doctor told me to pull on it. I hesitated and he said it was OK. He said, "Go ahead. It won't hurt her." I tugged on it and out came a beautiful chrysanthemum. It was gold with rust-colored flecks on it. I was puzzled but had a happy feeling. When I awoke, I had a tremendous feeling of peace and I knew that Milly's suffering was over. Just a few minutes later, Dick called to tell me that Milly had died that morning.

After the funeral, we went back to our home in Detroit. About an hour after we got home the doorbell rang. There was a florist's truck out in front and a potted plant was being delivered to our home. It was from a relative who could not attend the funeral. It was a beautiful gold chrysanthemum with rust colored flecks on it.

EPILOGUE

Now that you have read my stories, I hope you have come to some conclusions - whether there are ghosts, demons, spirits or Satanism at work, or whether there is life after death or not. Maybe you still believe the stories are a figment of some one's or my imagination; were we dreaming, were we on drugs and hallucinating, were we drunk, or are we just plain crazy.

If you are still uncertain of what to believe, let me add this one more incident which I heard on WJR Radio in Detroit on October 17, 1991.

It was written in the Southern Medical Journal that:

A medical mistake was made during an operation on a woman, which resulted in her death. After several minutes, the operating staff brought her back to life. when she awoke the following day, there were doctors and nurses at her bedside to tell her of her close call with death. She said she knew that she died because she hovered above the operating room table. They were all very skeptical until she started to describe what they were doing during her death. She told one doctor about the different colored socks he wore (he didn't want anyone to know this), and the others about their various expressions during the emergency, and who wore glasses, and who didn't.

The amazing part of this story is that she was blind!!! I will close with a quote:

> There are only two ways to live.
> One is though nothing is a miracle,
> the other is as if everything is.
>
> Albert Einstein

ABOUT THE AUTHOR

After military service in World War II, Ed Kwiatkowski, graduated from Central Michigan University in 1950 with a teaching degree in social studies, but opted to go on to the Detroit Fire Department. He also worked as a substitute teacher in the Detroit school system for twenty-three years on his days off. As he put it, "he fought fires one day, and 'kids' the next day." He retired from the fire department after thirty years service in 1980.

Soon after retiring, he got tired of being inactive. Within two years he got work as a bus tour director. For five years, he traveled all over the U.S. and Canada. He got "burned out" by having to make close schedules, living out of a suitcase, and being away from home for long periods of time.

He resumed teaching as a Driver Education teacher for another five years at a local high school, only to be "burned out" the second time, this time because too many of his students did not know their right hand from their left, which caused him near heart attacks when he told them to turn left, and they turned right.

He decided to write about what he loved to do, fire house and home style cooking. He wrote a humorous fire department cookbook, *Cooking with a Smile at the Fire House*. The vast popularity of it brought about its sequel.

Finally, having time on his hands, he decided to reveal his inner secrets about communicating with souls from the outer world, which mainly we refer to as "ghosts".

The author dares the reader after reading his book, not to believe in the hereafter. He feels you will have to sit down and strongly reflect on the subject, pass judgment on it if you never have before, and that your curiosity will be aroused as never before.

His short ghost stories are very convincing that there is such a life, because they show the interaction of humans and the other world after death.

It will unfold what is mystifying, unclear, baffling, and unexplainable. It will clarify what the scientific world is powerless to explain.

You will read about people who have great psychic abilities, and mediums who join the two worlds together.

It will fortify your beliefs, that there is something more than this life, and that you are watched and helped by those from beyond.

Printed in the United States
5486